INTER SECTION:

What teaching in one of the United States' most segregated school districts taught me about life, g(race), and education.

CHANDRA D. HAWKINS

ISBN-13: 9798832443621

To my Sparkling Scholars and Families:
It was my honor to be a part of your lives. My life
is forever changed because of it.

To my Mamo:
Whose love of teaching and desire to write a book
was passed on to her granddaughter.

TABLE OF CONTENTS

INTRODUCTION

When someone asks me how I came to be a teacher I generally start the conversation with a nuanced lead such as, "My journey in education isn't a typical one." To be completely fair, my journey to be a teacher is far from the typical "my mom was a teacher, and I grew up knowing I would one day be a teacher" storyline. My journey into and out of education has defined my entire life.

Throughout college, I would be asked by my professors, "Talk about a time a teacher inspired you." I couldn't really answer those questions. Not truly. I would be asked to think about what our classroom experiences were like in third, fifth, and seventh grades. I didn't have a traditional point of reference. I kept quiet, having nothing to say.

It had all been the same, mundane, endless, lonely, and sometimes horrifying experience. I was able to use the advantages of unstructured learning to pursue writing, flute, piano, watercolor, clothing, and home design. However, my homeschooling education lacked friendships, community, and teamwork. My homeschooling experience lacked diversity and exposure to those different from myself. I lacked real world experiences and real obstacles that would help me learn how to appreciate and respect those different from myself.

My journey to become a teacher was not a lateral one. Upon graduating high school, I found myself doing what I had been destined for and raised to do at the tender age of (barely) twenty: being a young, stay at home momma who had lost the opportunity to attend the Ivy League school I had once dreamt of. I lost my way for a few years.

As the pages unfold, you will see my struggle and what I know in my heart I was destined for, far beyond the patriarchal expectations of misogyny. I was destined to live this story in all its forms so that I could be an advocate for a system that when it is healthy and functioning well, it builds a generation, bonds a society, and brings together people. That is sadly not the case today.

This is the story of a teacher who was great and loved and knew how to build bridges across the Grand Canyon gaps in a child's education. It is also the story of a teacher who knew that her time was finished in the classroom, and it was time to share her story with the world. I share my story with the hope that through awareness we can begin to cultivate needed change. My prayer is that within the intersectionality of educational systems, we can find common ground, build something new and reimagined, and recognize that all children have the right to an education. This is after all, 2022.

The teacher shortage is looming into a massive problem our society will have to come together to solve. Teachers are tired, stressed, overworked, and looking for the last bit of oil in their lamps to keep burning. This is 2022.

Just last year we as a nation watched Diane Sawyer's *20/20* episode on the horrifying abuse that the Turpin children were subjected to under the guise of homeschooling. Homeschool students still face a system that is clearly broken and inadequate to catch the neglect and abuse that happens on a regular basis within these homes. This is 2022. The pandemic is still among us, and teachers and students are trying to continue life as normal in a system that wasn't designed for grace, tragedy, or trauma. Our educational system is crumbling, and lawmakers aren't hearing the drum beat of educators (and parents) across America: It's time for a change. The time is now.

Author's Note: All names have been changed to honor the privacy of individuals within. This is a memoir and as such, these are my experiences and perceptions from my unique vantage point. Resemblance is coincidental, and details have been changed or added to aid in the storytelling of this memoir, while preserving the integrity of my story.

A REAM OF PAPER

I pulled out of the parking lot, with tears streaming down my cheeks and my GMC Acadia packed tightly with books, a rocking chair, and everything that I had bought to supply my classroom, that my view was obstructed. My car smelled like my life for the last two years. My life had been full of beautiful people, hard things, grit, and love. Relief washed over me as I put on my turn signal. Waves of grief hit so hard it shocked me with the weight of it, as I began to turn the corner. I had done the hard thing, the impossible even. I had survived my first two years of teaching in one of the nation's most racially segregated school districts. Perhaps more astonishing was that I emerged stronger, more resilient, transformed, and forever changed. My life has been full of the impossibly difficult.

The clean, crisp modern brick building stood in contrast to the stately, established oak trees. The building looked as if it had seen and heard everything in the span of her stately years, inherently wise to the ways of man and good at listening. The salmon-colored brick looked young and fresh, similar to how the carefree voices of the children playing on the bright blue playground just beyond the overgrown shrubs and grasses, sounded. This contrast of old and new would prove to be poetic in its irony. I took a deep breath, attempting to shake my nerves. I was dressed for power, with white pants and a black trench coat.

In my mind, dressing the part helped to increase my confidence but inside, I felt about as strong as St. Louis' gooey butter cake.

I had been preparing for this moment for years. I pulled my little white Kia Spectra into the parking space and grabbed my portfolio. One of the things that my colleagues and I heard while we were in college was to bring our portfolio into an interview. A portfolio was a compilation of documents, sample lesson plans, and artifacts, all housed within a 3-ring binder. While in college, I was a determined student, and a self-admitted over-achiever. I found achieving the next grade and getting positive feedback addictive. I hadn't had that affirmation during my homeschool experience. I had brought my portfolio with me into my interview. It weighed at least five pounds and I had taken special care to create a scrapbooking page that allowed my interviewers to see a small snippet of what they could expect from me just in case it wasn't looked at. Bunnies, birch trees, mushrooms, bunting draped between two trees adorned the front cover. Visions of what I hoped my classroom would one day look like. My credentials were typed in my preferred font, Harrington. I was most proud of my classroom management plan. The affirmation that "it was the best I have ever seen" from a former professor and school superintendent of a large district in the St. Louis metro area became a sincere source of pride in my accomplishments.

I had completed my college classes a couple of weeks prior and found myself interviewing for my next dream:

a classroom of my own. The position was for teaching first graders.

The insane factor was that I hadn't even walked for graduation nor had my degree conferred yet.

I was preparing myself that I would have to work my way into a classroom of my own, likely substitute teaching before that would happen. Still, the fact that I had this opportunity to interview instilled a quiet confidence within me. My graduation ceremony wasn't for another month. I had spent four years in school hearing how stiff the competition would be in terms of landing an interview, let alone a job. I was content to have the experience to interview because I knew that it would sharpen me. But I also believed that I was the best candidate for this job and had a heart full of passion to advocate for students.

I opened my car door, grabbed my teaching portfolio, along with extra copies of my resume printed off on high quality paper. I bravely stepped onto the stifling, sulfur smelling, newly paved asphalt. I straightened my white pants and black blazer. After smoothing my hair but not the butterflies that had made their home in my midsection, I was as ready as I would ever be.

It wasn't the first time I had been here, in this place. I had come a week earlier for round two. The first round was passing a lengthy phone interview where I was asked questions about my teaching philosophy, and I had made sure to be assertive and share how I had the ability to move students and improve scores while student teaching. They called back later that day to ask me to return to teach a lesson.

All of my college coursework had not prepared me for this process. I felt like I was in a pressure-cooker. The stress of job performance was eminent and real. All for a $40,000 a year opportunity to transform lives and have a lasting impact. This was what education was about, I was sure of it.

I walked into the classroom where I was going to teach a math lesson to first graders with a Smartboard that wasn't too smart. We couldn't get it to work, despite two other staff members troubleshooting. Two guys from technology were called into problem solve. I abandoned my original plan on the fly and gathered this class of unknown children around me on the carpet. I made myself at home, pulling out manipulatives and anchor chart paper while these impressionable little people stared at me. And then I freaked out.

No one told me that this lesson would be videotaped and analyzed by several staff members. The pressure to perform was unreal and the perfectionist within became impossible to appease from that moment. I made sure that I had studied the website copiously. My entire lesson was a blur, and the only thing I remembered about it was making sure that I worked the camera angles. I made it a point to ensure the lens captured my skills in working with ESL students. Rather than get completely flustered, I thrived under the pressure. Considering my story, it wasn't surprising or shocking.

I felt the lesson went well, but the room was not set up to teach the way that I liked; conversational, relational, and enough floor space for everyone to be gathered in a circle. Mel, the Instructional Coach who had initially interviewed me on the phone, walked me out when it was over and asked me to watch a 4o minute video of a different lesson and then respond to prompts through writing. I was relieved to be asked to showcase my writing abilities.

I knew I could nail this piece. I was able to ask to meet with the principal after I had completed every task and she and I had a positive conversation. I asked her how many other candidates I was up against. She casually turned behind her and placed her hand on a stack of papers.

"Well, Ms. Hawkins, this is your competition."

"*All* of them?" I said rather incredulously.

"Yes, probably 800 applicants we have reviewed. We are trying to narrow it down."

I didn't know what to say so I switched the topic to talking about data. I was asked to come back for the final round of interviews before the day was over. Round three and what felt like the opportunity of a lifetime was now waiting for me just inside the school on this day that I donned my black and white pants suit. I pushed through the stainless-steel doors, the glass panes smudged with the traces of the children who called this place home for eight hours a day, went into the office and waited.

I heard the dismissal bells going off and the kids sounded like the constant buzz of a beehive, but louder. It felt alive and electric, kids clapping rhythmically and talking in a way that felt like they were intensified. They were fired up; they were going home.

I was escorted into the conference room as the staff frantically tried to get the copier to work to print off more copies of their interview questions for the twelve people who were waiting to meet me in the conference room. My principal laughed it off. I wasn't worried. I was confident that I had this job. I felt that this was the next part of my calling.

I knew that if I was meant to be here in this place and impact the lives of the students and their parents, that God would make it happen.

Plus, it's kind of hard not to be confident when you know you just beat out 800 other people who wanted the same opportunity to interview in front of the panel. The interview could not have gone better. I was confident, made them laugh, laughed with them, answered their questions eloquently, made eye contact, and asked a few questions myself. I was naive, but I felt in my gut that this was where I was meant to be. I was called to be here.

I wasn't wrong. I was offered the job the very next day. I was blown away by God's grace. In an entire ream of paper, I was the one that they had chosen. Myself, and few others who would soon fill my life. My destiny and purpose, my why, was coming to fruition. I anxiously awaited the day when I could walk into the school and meet the students who were going to become a part of my life. Key word there is anxiously. Nothing spells worry and anxiety like a first-year teacher, teaching in a high stakes district, quite like that.

THE WONDER YEARS

"Growing up happens in a heartbeat.
One day you're in diapers, the next day you're gone.
But the memories of childhood stay with you for the long
haul. And the thing is, after all these years, I still look
back, with wonder."
-Kevin Savage, <u>The Wonder Years</u>

Nestled in the heart of Con-Agra territory, wound between the Nebraska and Missouri Rivers on the northwest edge of Missouri, and situated among the ancient rolling hills and plains of the former Otoe tribe is where my life began. A tiny town of population 600.

Down the main street you will find a gas station that is still full-service. The different shades of blue, with yellow and red signs make it appear larger than it is. The men match the station in their dusty Dickies coveralls and Pioneer ballcaps, smudged with oil and grease, grime permanently caked on their hands and the guy who managed it has an overgrown sandy color mustache. His mustache matches the dust that has covered the station from the combines, tractors, and semis that roll through the main street to get to the nearest highway, taking the nation's food supply to the masses.

Next to the gas station, just down the street on the corner is the town grocery store. There used to be three, but there's only one now. It's changed hands over the years, sometimes it's locally owned and operated, other times it's an outsider, as the locals say. Walking in through the manual glass door you hear the little bell jingle on the door, and you see the meat counter at the back. The smell of musty old carpet strikes you as you enter this postage-stamp sized store and smell the homegrown produce that is just to the left. The freshest cuts of beef and pork are sold here at the meat counter in the very back of the store. This little mom and pop grocery store has nearly anything that you might need, so making the 45-minute trip to St. Joseph wasn't usually necessary. Unless you were my grandma who was the best chef in a dozen counties. My grandpa went on more grocery store trips than anyone I'd ever seen. The conveyor belt in the checkout lane moves with a slow, herky-jerky motion that reminds you that time sometimes can appear to stand still. It's sleepy and laid back, just like Fairfax.

Across the street from the corner grocery store, is Roger's Pharmacy. It doesn't look like much because the window is covered in dust and the lighting is pretty poor. It's dark inside. This place develops film and pictures, sells Strawberry Shortcake dolls and furniture for the Berry Happy Home, matchbox cars, He-Man figurines, an assortment of candy, and is a place to fill the doctor's prescriptions from the Fairfax Memorial Hospital that my great-grandpa Hawkins helped to bring to the town.

First Community Bank is also next door to Roger's. It's dark inside, with fancy brown carpet that has a Spanish-motif design on the floor. It smells like new money and ink pens, is chilly, and I never tired of the Dum-Dums, always hoping for watermelon. Going to the bank was nearly a half day excursion, everyone had a story to tell. Santa always made an appearance in the lobby, every December. I think my picture with Santa was in the Fairfax Forum newspaper every year until we moved.

My grandparents were good friends with the owners and editors of the local newspaper, and they made sure that my silly sayings somehow made their way into the Forum. Their favorite one was the one where I told the pastor during a children's sermon who was intentionally messing up a retelling of a parable for dramatic effect, "Man, he sure keeps messin' this up!" My favorite was remembering telling the editor of the newspaper, at the grocery store, he "looked like Santa Clause." Pretty sure that story didn't make the cut.

There's a park in the center of town, a heating and cooling store, a fabric store where my Grammy would buy her patterns, fabric, and buttons, the Daybreak Cafe' where the old men gather for black coffee and gossip, beauty parlors, and a large farm store that sells John Deere and International Harvester machinery. The Dairy Diner is the talk of the town and it's only open from April-September. They serve the best pork tenderloin sandwiches, and my favorite is their cherry dipped soft serve cone. Just up the road before you get to the main part of town is the school. It's a big part of my family history and my Grampy was the Principal, Athletic Director, football, and basketball coach. My aunt worked there as a teacher before she became the Elementary school principal.

Just beyond the boundaries of town, are the hundreds of acres of peaceful, rolling hills and coveted farm ground. About five miles outside of town, is where my grandparents lived; down a gravel road, over an old, rusty bridge, around a bend, past Walkup's Grove Cemetery, and down a hill. It's a story and a half white farmhouse, modest. There's a cellar with a white door, oversized red barn, small white garden shed, detached two car garage, and a large driveway big enough for Granddad's combine and pickup truck. If you go back up the road, over the bridge there's a tiny red stucco house overshadowed by an oak tree that has likely been there since the Native Americans who once claimed this land, lived. The house belongs to my Granddad, happily situated on his 900-acre farm. This is the home of my childhood before we moved away, just a quarter mile from my dad's parents.

My early childhood was idyllic. In many ways, the memories that were woven into the fabric of my heart and life provided a safe haven from the unintended trauma that I would later experience. My life was filled with my four grandparents, four cousins, seven aunts and uncles, four great-grandparents, and countless extended family. I can't remember a day when I didn't have an extended family member in my life, for the first five years of my life.

I don't remember much about winter, but spring was a time of awakening on the farm. Mamo and Granddad's farm woke up from its slumber. Mamo would be working the soil in her strawberry bed; Granddad would be covered in dirt dust from planting corn and soybeans in the fields. The momma cats would begin to have their kittens, and though wild, it never stopped me from chasing them down and being known as, "The Kitten

Tamer." I would smother those poor creatures with love until they had no choice but to purr. The number of scratches didn't faze me. I would carry those poor fluff balls around in an empty purse, wrap them up in old towels, and refuse to let them out of my sight. Some days, we would take them home to the Little Red House where I would dress them up in My Little Pony clothes. They were fed with kitten formula and kitten bottles. They lived the life of luxury on those green acres.

Easter was a beautiful time, Mamo's irises would be blooming, and they looked like Monet's Water Lilies in my mind. An annual feathered visitor, a Baltimore Oriole returned to build its nest above the elm tree. The bobwhite quail would be calling, and one year we found a nest of quail babies that we rescued from Momma Cat's hunting prowess. Dying Easter eggs was a rite of childhood, and it was something that I did with both sets of grandparents. Mamo always got the fancy sets; Grandma was simpler and got the solid colors. Easter also meant fancy clothes and Sunday service, deviled eggs, and ham. Spring also meant mushroom hunting for morels with Grandma which also meant learning how to pee in the woods. It meant picking rhubarb in Grammy's backyard and scooping up a plastic yogurt container of peanut M&Ms out of her refrigerator.

Summer was lazy, and loud. The crickets, cicadas, and birds were a near constant roar in the background. Pickup trucks and tractors, kicking up dust clouds behind them, were in constant motion, adding to the catatonic orchestra. With Grandma, summer meant elaborate laundry days, where clothes were hung out to dry and sometimes, we got out Grandma Lizzie's wringer-washer and did everything by hand. It meant unsweet instant Lipton tea on the front porch while Grandma smoked her cigarette, the only time she ever sat still. Summer was synonymous with open windows, crowing roosters, homegrown tomatoes, and electric fans. Summer was when Mamo would sit under the shade trees and watch us kids play basketball on the driveway or sing us songs. Cooling off was popsicles, swimming in the cow's water tank, playing in the hose, or occasionally, the slip-n-slide. Shucking sweet corn out of the back of a pick-up truck or shelling peas, canning produce, and watching game shows when it got too hot outside was a daily part of life.

Fall was beautiful and busy. The harvesters were out in full force, with Granddad often pulling into the driveway with his harvester full of soybeans. Mamo and I would scoop out handfuls of freshly hulled soybeans and eat them one by one. Nothing tasted fresher, more rewarding, or earthy than those soybeans. The maple tree north of Mamo and Granddad's house would turn a brilliant orangish-red. Mamo loved fall, I think it reminded her of the circadian rhythm of going back to school and teaching in her one room schoolhouse, Cherry Dale. Halloween was a time of going to Marianne and Harold's haunted barn, where Grandma dressed up as the scariest Frankenstein ever. My cousin Amber and I screamed bloody murder and were so terrified our moms told Grandma to take off her mask. That mask was somehow resurrected every year thereafter, and it was no less terrifying with the passage of time. Halloween was a time of getting the best homemade popcorn balls from Grandma and driving to

Mamo and Granddad's so we could fill our bags with candy and the Pinterest-worthy treat bags (those were my favorite). One year, we had a huge Halloween party at the Little Red House and our old barn caught on fire. It was destroyed before the volunteer fire department could put it out.

Small town autumn was a time of plenty. Thanksgiving was a feast and filled to the brim with family. It was in November that my dad announced that after completing his college degree, he would be moving to St. Louis. He never wanted to be a "dirt farmer" and wanted to chase his dreams of business in the city. It was near devastation to my grandparents, no one from this corner of the world had ever dared to leave for something so far away and unknown.

Right before we moved in late July of 1986, Granddad built a treehouse in the apple tree. Built is a loose word, Granddad could run a productive farm, but he was not good with tools. It was sturdy enough for me, and my other two cousins, my two-year-old brother had stayed home. We climbed up onto the platform and had a picnic in that apple tree, that last night before we moved. The fireflies were extra memorable, and our giggles rang out across the farm. I knew Granddad built it for Mamo, not for us. She knew, unlike me, that nothing would ever be the same again.

My childhood in the city of St. Louis stood in stark contrast to the idyllic backdrop of Fairfax. It was different, not bad, but different. A park-like yard. Neighbors on either side. A busy intersection. Cars, mufflers falling off, ambulances. The promise of going to the elementary school down the street and getting on the bus with my next-door neighbor friend, Mara was an exciting change. She was the same age as me, just two months older. We were both blonde haired, blue eyed, French braid wearing, girls who loved roller skates, Strawberry Shortcake, and drawing. We were best friends for a while- at least, until things began to change.

We would spend hours together that summer, playing with our Strawberry Shortcake and Barbie collections. We would color on the driveway. We would make perler beads and friendship bracelet crafts. And together, we dreamed of backpacks, the bus stop, and new friends we would make in kindergarten. I was all enrolled and ready to attend McKelvey Elementary School, riding bus 27.

The first day of school came upon me and I hid. I remember hearing my mom on the phone, speaking with the office.

"Yes, hello? This is Karen. I am calling because my daughter, Chandra Hawkins was supposed to get on the bus this morning and she will not be attending school; she will be homeschooled."

I was under the desk in the kitchen- hiding, in a safe space. It was dark. I was enclosed on three walls and could only see out the front through the chair legs. The yellow light cast from the light in the kitchen felt like sunshine to my eyes. My mom and the secretary went back and forth exchanging information and my life, as I knew it, would never be the same again.

CULT(ISH)

My life as a child pioneer of the homeschooling movement of the 80's was something akin to a mixture of the Twilight Zone and feeling like I was observing everyone and everything around me as though I were a fly on the wall. I was blessed- or cursed? - with a photographic memory. I remember how things look, feel, patterns of fabrics, time of year, dates, words, expressions. All of it. Mamo used to tell me I had a memory like an elephant and that I got my memory from her.

It was a few weeks before my mom's decision to begin homeschooling me, that she was introduced to Jim and Laura Rodgers. They were introduced at a local church we began attending through another family who were also beginning to homeschool their children. Jim and Laura Rodgers were the architects of the homeschooling law in the State of Missouri, and it was that moment that became the first steppingstone into the grass-roots movement of homeschooling for my family. I remember going over to their house for Sunday dinner after church. While nothing remarkable happened, I remember astutely thinking, *Mr. and Mrs. Rodgers say they love kids, but they don't feel very loving.* I was afraid to be myself, fearful of reprimands and scornful gazes should

I stray into childlike ways. It was there that my mom was first introduced to a support group for homeschooling families and introduced to new up-and-coming leaders and lobbyists for homeschooling families' rights.

I still remember the first time I met the Winters family. My mom needed information on the homeschooling law, the rights of homeschoolers, and how to begin the planning process of educating a young child- in the days before the plethora of information was at your fingertips. The only way to get resources was to meet face to face, so off we went to the Winters house.

We walked up the sidewalk that cut through the center of their lawn like the insides of a peanut butter and jelly sandwich. White bridal spirea bloomed on either side of the wide light-mauve, gray stairway leading to the door. It was a large, deep mauve home, painted and immaculately kept gracious windows on either side with a generous front porch, just off St. Louis Avenue, in Ferguson, MO. How little did I know that the place I would spend much of my St. Louis childhood would later point to a deeper story of racism and supremacy in the fabric of our nation's history.

Cynthia answered the door, greeting us with a charming, charismatic smile and twinkly eyes that squinted when she laughed. Her waist-length, wavy, chestnut brown hair was pulled half-way back out of her eyes. Behind her knee-length shorts a copy-cat version of myself: another blonde haired, blue eye girl.

"Come on in. Can I get you something to drink?" Cynthia asked my mom as we were shown to the living room. She brought back some lemonade for my mom as my little brother, and I sat on the floor. She introduced her daughter, Eliza, to me.

"Why don't you take Chandra back to your room and you can play back there while Mrs. Hawkins and I talk?" She said to Eliza. "Just be careful you don't wake Elise up."

I was taken back to a beautiful bedroom. Eyelet curtains and a ruffly bedspread adorned the room. A porcelain doll was in the center of the bed, her blue eyes and ringlets looking so...perfected. Everything was immaculate and girly. It was exactly how I wanted my bedroom to be. We sat on the floor and began playing with dolls. Hours went by and we felt we were just getting started. Our moms were laughing in the living room. Elise woke up and she was exactly how Shirley Temple would have looked like a baby: happy, tawny, with perfect ringlets and blue silver-dollar sized eyes. We entertained Elise and Malachi and it felt like we had been separated at birth, newly reunited. Eliza and I, playing as though we'd known each other for our entire lives basking in the sunny warmth of the smoky blue bedroom carpet. Our moms, whose conversation and levity didn't cease, began fostering a life-changing friendship. We were there until dinner.

And so, it began.

The years went by and with them, change replaced familiarity. Though shocking at first, change becomes your normal. Change becomes what you get used to after a while, replacing stability with frequent disruptions to routine. It wasn't long after my new ABeka textbooks and readers arrived, that mom took me to the basement to sort through my toy box.

I loved this toybox. It was a flimsily made 1980's MDF model. It had super bright, Barney purple, grass green, and black and white sketches on the sides. The children imprinted on the sides looked something akin to a Stephen King cinematic masterpiece. The front had a sliding door, the same jarring grass green as the drawings of the kids in the park on the sides of the box. There was a small, narrow shelf on the top, similar to a little bookshelf. Nothing ever seemed to fit on those top shelves though. Everything ended up in the storage compartment, like an island for lost and forgotten toys.

There we were, sitting on the cold basement floor, taking my toys out one by one and sorting through them. I had a red backpack full of Barbies, My Little Ponies scattered around, Rainbow Brite dolls, Care Bears, and other iconic vestiges of the 1980's all hidden inside this Stephen King toybox. There was no warning, no subtle changes in conversation or viewpoints on my toys, only what appeared to my seven-year-old self to be sudden and unexpected.

My mom sat me down and looked me in the eyes, cold, calculating- lacking compassion and a nurturing instinct.

"Do you know what magic is?" my mother asked me, devoid of all inflection.

"Nooo," my seven-year-old self replied.

"It's where Satan uses power over things to try to come into your home. Satan wants to scare you and try to make you do things you shouldn't. Magic is evil. We don't want Satan in our house, so we are getting rid of things he loves."

My eyes went wide. I had been raised in Sunday School and church; I knew who Satan was. Every seven-year-old sees the world in black and white, with the absence of gray. They need concrete examples to process and make sense of their world. Suddenly, my toys felt evil. They felt corrupted, tainted, and scary. I didn't want Satan to find me or get to me through my toys. Yet I loved my toys. We had very little money, and the toys I had I treasured. I was never one to draw on my dolls or cut their hair because I knew that the implication of that meant they could not be replaced. This didn't feel right, and I was instantly conflicted, sorting through the reality of what I felt against the powerful tug of brainwashing. How could these toys which had brought me happiness be so evil? How? To fight was futile, but I could feel the tears welling up in my eyes. Hot steaming tears slid down my cheeks as we purged our home of demonic influences.

The first thing we sorted through was the colorful array of the My Little Pony collection. Sundance, Moonbeam, Pegasus, Gusty, my pair of twin baby unicorns with the purple and red manes...gone. Sorted into the pile of demon-possessed, placed in a black Hefty bag so that they could not be looked at again. I made the argument that Bow Tie and Applejack and Puddles were just colorful horses, with no wings or magical horns. My mom allowed them to remain behind. I placed them on the small shelf and lined them up.

I was ok with giving up Rainbow Brite because I only had one doll, though secretly I wanted to ask for more on my next birthday. I was too afraid to ask for more because I knew we didn't have money. Mara had all of them and they were so much fun to play with. I knew we didn't have the money for them, usually Christmas meant asking for things like clothes and shoes. Looming in the background was my red backpack and I dreaded it. I said goodbye to my Care Bears. My head was spinning- if that's a thing seven-year-old selves do. I was trying to process losing the connectedness I felt to my toys. The only other time I could remember this feeling of loss was when we moved to St. Louis from Fairfax. I had an emotional connection to my toys, much in the same way as I felt a strong emotional connection to my grandparents. My parents did not provide the emotional connection I needed, so I sought it from other sources. My toys were a source of safety amongst brokenness.

My mom pulled out the Barbies and asked me to line them up on the floor. They looked like a firing squad. The clothing and accessories were pulled out, laid in a pile underneath their feet.

Every Barbie was held up and examined. I was confused- Barbies weren't magic. But they did contain a powerful element: empowering young girls to feel beautiful, sexy, confident, and capable. The magic of beautiful womanhood would be something I would be asked to do without. The next few minutes were spent in Mom selecting Barbies from the lineup, inspecting them, and informing me how certain outfits the Barbies wore were worldly, immodest, suggestive, and drawing too much attention to themselves. Ken was placed in the black trash bag. Purple and blue dresses, white formal gowns, high heels. *Gone.* Workout Barbie, Loving You Barbie, Day to Night, Fashion Jeans Barbie. *Gone.* Tears filled my big blue eyes and spilled down onto the former doll collection. Angel Face Barbie remained, along with one Skipper doll and The Heart Family.

I surveyed my remaining toys. Odds and ends, bits and pieces remained. Toy collections were ravished, skeletons of what once was. This was the first of a calculated move to brainwash me into believing that things and outside influences would cause me to become bad, sinful, and worldly and that in order to remain pure and holy, I had to keep myself unstained from the world.

A silver lining came that same summer when my dream of having a cat of my very own came true. Grandma and Grandpa's cat, Dummy (aptly named for her ability to be the neighborhood hoe), had a beautiful set of kittens. I picked out this beautiful, long-haired, white, and gray kitten whom we named Whitey Herzog. He became my inseparable friend. It was never a dog who was my best friend. It was a cat, who became my guardian angel and sidekick who never once left my side. He witnessed every imaginary world, every tear that fell as I cried myself to sleep, and every prayer I prayed.

Spending the days at the Winters house on St. Louis Avenue in Ferguson shaped my world and contributed to the brainwashing of the cult that raised me. Little would I know that the neighborhood in which I spent a vast majority of my time just 26 years later, would be the scene of national news, drawing attention to the racism that I had seen cultivated on these streets. Racism was indeed homegrown.

It became increasingly hard to socialize with kids in the neighborhood. Mara and I drifted apart as she began to go to school. When the toys you play with are evil, suddenly, the toys your friends play with and own are evil, too. I was no longer allowed to go inside Mara's home, as there might be influences of evil there such as television programming or toys that I wasn't allowed to play with. My playmates came more and more from increasingly homogeneous circles who looked, dressed, thought, and worshiped like our family. Even my cousins became distanced, judgment setting in as a way to protect myself from feeling so completely awkward.

I remember drinking this Kool-Aid. When cousins or neighbors would ask, "Why can't you watch She-ra? Punky Brewster? Full House?" the response would be cold, calculated, rehearsed like the tone I had been taught with.

"Because they are worldly. They do things that are sinful," I would regurgitate with robotic accuracy. I never believed the lies I restated but I had no explanation as to why I couldn't watch these seemingly harmless shows.

My birthday was in the heat of summer. Most kids, I have since learned as a teacher, love a summer birthday. No school, not a care in the world, and endless opportunities for finding things to do. I grew to hate it.

I was a natural-born swimmer. I loved water, water sports, and my adorable Lisa Frank snow leopard swimming suit with the ruffle trim. Little Mermaid was released in 1989, just after I turned eight and just as my world was rapidly changing. I was still able to go and watch it in the theater with Mara and her mom, but that was short lived when my mom realized that Ariel was a girl striving to break free from her father's rule. I loved her. Somewhere deep inside was my desire to break free, inspired by a strong-willed girl.

The following summer, I remember playing in the streets of Ferguson, across from the post office, having a water hose fight with Eliza, our younger siblings, and a couple of neighborhood girls. It was a hot, humid St. Louis day. Anyone who is from St. Louis knows that the humidity is something that is notable and oppressive. Once it sets in, it is a rare thing to get a break from it, even at night. We eagerly await the arrival of fall when we feel relief, like drinking a Coke in a glass that's beaded over from the ice. The water today felt glorious.

We went in to grab a popsicle. As we drip-dried off on the front porch, I overheard my mom and Cynthia through the open windows over our giggles, noisy car mufflers, and the *crick-crick-criiick* of the porch swing. My bare feet drug across the painted wood floor. I loved to trace the lines on the boards with my toes, so smooth and cool.

"You know that going to public swimming pools is not a good thing, don't you?" Cynthia asked, placing just the right amount of inflection on the word, know. We had planned to go to the local public swimming pool later that afternoon.

"N-nnoo. Why?" my mom hesitated, confused.

"Black people go there, and they have *AIDS.*"

At the height of the AIDS epidemic and awareness campaign, AIDS was a source of national news. Misinformation, racism, and colorism were abundant. The soil was ripe to spread lies and hatred. Fear was the water that sprouted these seeds of racism.

Cynthia continued in her voice, stern, and firm. "You can get AIDS from the swimming pool in the water. You can get it from toilet seats. Any surface you share, you can get AIDS from. You don't want Chandra and Malachi to get AIDS, do you?"

This is how, in part, Cynthia created a racist cult where we lived in constant fear of outside influences. Gaslighting, warping sense of logic, reason, and science in favor of emotional alarm and over-protection. Mom was always naive, a follower and never sure of herself. All it took was questions in the form of concern and bathed in manipulation and seeds of doubt to tailspin us further into this rabbit hole. The conversation carried on, with Mom being the dutiful pupil. Cynthia continued to discuss the dangers of public pools: how immodest women were and how you were likely to have men waiting to rape little girls in the bathrooms. She fed these lies with such confidence and self-assuredness that it would have felt silly of someone to question what she said for even a moment.

I grew up watching my cousins and next-door neighbor go to the public swimming pool while I stayed home. Safe. Protected. Unstained.

My mom made my homemade swimming suit and when I outgrew that, I just didn't care. I remembered how much I adored the swimming pool, swimming like the little mermaid I fantasized I was. I relegated myself to baggy, soggy t-shirts and shorts. I grew to hate summer and all things water related. I felt frumpy and awkward in my tee shirts and shorts. I couldn't move my body gracefully and it didn't matter anyway. The hose was no longer fun, and the pool was no longer an option.

As the seasons unfurled from summer to autumn and winter, my world became increasingly "unsafe." When Northwest Plaza was remodeled, the largest mall in St.

Louis at the time, complete with video arcades, a massive food court, movie theater, and all the trending flagship stores, after going there a few times with cousins who came in to visit from Fairfax- the fun in life stopped, again, abruptly.

There had been an armed robbery at the mall, shortly after it had opened. In St. Louis, crime is something we have grown accustomed to. It's seeped in racial and fiscal segregation. Its origin is complex and not well understood. After the robbery, we quit going to the mall and if we went, we were strategic about staying away from "that side." Black men were the cause of the crime and robbery, according to my mom. We had to stay safe, we had to avoid the area.

Trips downtown to Union Station dwindled as more people of color moved in. Too many gangs, again, too many black men, and "thugs." The last trip I took to Union Station was at Christmastime. It remains a beautiful place at Christmastime, full of magical twinkly lights, greenery, festive trees, and glittery ornaments. We had just come out of a hat store where Eliza and I had chosen Christmas presents for each other. There were people everywhere, but Cynthia and my mom claimed that there were two groups of black men walking on either side of the station, sporting gang colors. We were told this was now unsafe and that we needed to leave. We never went back. It was years before I returned as an adult and even then, I wasn't untainted by the racism I was taught.

My mom became further and further immersed into a phrase I heard much of my life which called, "Growing The Movement." This phrase happened organically, as a result of the grass-roots nature of homeschooling back in the days when people questioned why children were being seen in public places during school hours. I remember the stares of people, looking deep into my eyes in those early days, especially grocery store clerks. Going into Shop N Save with my mom was part of home economics and math class, although the only thing I ever learned was how to select produce and how to read labels.

Often the conversations would revolve around if we were happy and liked being at home all day. I lied. You can't tell your truth when your parents are right there next to you, ensuring you confirm to them that you are indeed happy with your school. To bear the weight of lying to protect your parent's image is a burden no child should have to endure. It changes your psyche; it messes with your entire perception of the world around you.

I knew I hated homeschooling. I wanted to go to school, have a lunch box, go shopping for back-to-school clothes like my cousins. I wanted friends more than anything else in the world. I was lonely, spending days in my room playing with dolls, counting the days to the next time I'd get to see Eliza or Michele or Lindsey. I wanted to learn.

Back in the days before the internet and email, the phone tree was the only way that information could get passed quickly from person to person. Much legislation was attempted to be passed in the 1980's and 1990's, bills that were drafted designed to increase homeschool accountability. These bills were sadly defeated many times over until people became accustomed to the homeschooling movement as somehow an oddly normalized part of American society. The phone tree took up hours of time and Cynthia appointed my mom with this task as a part of protecting and growing The Movement. When Mom proved successful in this, Cynthia appointed Mom to be in charge of educating new homeschoolers on the law in Missouri, informing them of their legal rights and obligations. Hours turned into entire days, which we then know what those days turned in to.

I grew up listening to the same mantra, given to a new person who was inquiring about homeschooling. You don't let anyone into your house if a family member calls Child Protective Services. The only person who has the right to see how many hours you logged for instruction, or your lesson plans are the attorney general. If a member of CPS shows up at your door, you call your local homeschooling support group leader and refuse to let them in. The need to protect parents and their right to homeschool was the only thing that was important, not the fact that concerned family, friends, and neighbors were wondering about the child's welfare. CPS became the boogieman. They became the entity who would show up, "falsely" accuse you of child neglect or abuse and strived to break up families. They were the entity with whom it appeared we went to war with daily.

Mamo had been a teacher in a one room schoolhouse, in a charming schoolhouse called Cherry Dale. She loved her students and teaching. She would often ask me things around the kitchen table when we were up in Fairfax to gauge what I was being taught. She never questioned me around my mom.

"Do you know your times tables yet?" She asked me one morning over my bowl of Fruit Loops and orange juice. I never got Fruit Loops at home and for some reason, her orange juice was so much better in her little yellow cups.

"Times tables? Oh yeah." I proceeded to read the clocks in the kitchen.

"No, I mean like 2x2 and '4 and 4 fell on the floor, pick them up and they are 64.'" She was concerned, her voice laced with worry. I was in fifth grade.

I felt so much shame in knowing that while I was a prolific reader and knew more history than most children my age, I was completely lost in math and science. The fun volcanos and building habitats? I never did those. I completed four and a half math textbooks by the time I graduated high school. I never completed a single science textbook, but I had read the original Magna Charta before I was thirteen.

When Mamo would question me on something and I didn't know what it was, I would go home in tears. In desperation, I would attempt to compel my mom to get off the phone and teach me what I didn't know and understand. These conversations would end fruitless and ultimately in frustration for me.

I eventually learned my multiplication facts, by the end of fifth grade and because I learned them, though not well, that would be considered a success story.

THE REMNANT

*"The worst of all fears
is the fear of living."*
-Theodore Roosevelt

Fear increased. My world became smaller, darker, and terrifying.

Conversations began about impending doom, the end of the world and something called Y2k. The government was predicted to take over, Jesus was returning, the world was ending. Preparations began in 1997. Centered around this catastrophic event was the idea that in order to be preserved in the return of Christ, you must be a "true" homeschooler. These true homeschoolers were the ones who were God's people, His Remnant, the chosen ones.

We were the ones who would be spared from a Government takeover and the ones who would be raptured. The days and times were unknown when Jesus would return, we had to be prepared to run and flee at a moment's notice. Prepared for our government to come and roll in on us, like they did in Tiananmen Square.

The whirlwind of preparation that happened was dizzying and horrifying. I lived in constant fear. Food began to get stockpiled in our pantry, food we could not eat and had to save. The money that could have been used to ensure that my brother and I didn't go to bed with growling stomachs was used towards prepping; beans, rice, extra water, plastic wrap for chemical warfare, plywood to board up windows. To have received help in the form of governmental assistance was forbidden by The Remnant because the government was thought to track you and we lived in fear that they would report families for child abuse and neglect. Food stamps were never an option or consideration for us.

I was hungry more times during the week than not. My shoes never fit, and I would wear the same pair several years in a row, stuffing the ends with toilet paper and by the time the shoes actually fit, they looked crusty and worn down. I hated my feet because of how self-conscious I felt, wearing shoes so much larger than I needed. The clothes I had were ill fitting and out of style, modest and homely, sometimes homemade. I would never experience the joy of expressing myself through fashion until I became much older, earning my own money. I would never know what it meant to not be hungry, or be afraid of being hungry, until I lived on my own. We were the forgotten children. Social services didn't know we existed. We slipped through the cracks, completely out of sight to society and to support systems. I often fantasized about what I would say and what my life would have looked like if a social worker knocked on our door. I fantasized about that scenario at least once a week.

Only "true homeschoolers" would be the ones who would be saved when Y2K hit, or so The Movement thought. Being a true homeschooler was someone who was white presenting, committed to every homeschool support group activity and meeting, no involvement with worldly activities like youth group or age segregated Sunday schools, sports, or dual enrollment with a local public school. If you followed these steps rigorously and faithfully, you were considered a true homeschooler. You were a part of the Movement, one of the faithful among the Remnant.

It was odd, this idea that the church would somehow corrupt young people. I grew up going to Sunday school *with* my parents. I felt like a social outcast. There was one other family whose boys did not attend traditional Sunday school with their peers. The boys' father was a U.S. Congressman, and their family was also a devoutly religious homeschool family. Their family was revered and yet, they hid their oldest son from the public eye due to his mental health issues that went largely untreated. It was an odd experience, going to Sunday School with one's parents. We would file in, avoiding eye contact, knowing that the adults who watched you come in and sit with your parents pitied us. I hated being looked at. I felt like I was some sort of social experiment.

As Y2K neared, my dad and mom began to purchase gold and priced guns and ammunition. Dad already had a .357 and bought a shotgun to have on hand. They discussed plans to move back to Fairfax if things got really bad. The Winters were stockpiling gold bars, handguns, pistols, AK-47s and other assault rifles. They were building a bunker and commune, their desire to move all true homeschoolers to their family farm in the middle of rural Missouri. Militia signups for the Missouri Mountainman Militia began to appear at every support group meeting. Signing up was heavily encouraged.

Things began to turn inward as we feared what would happen in the outside world. Fear was our guidepost, the deceptive light that led us into the depths of a grim hallway leading nowhere. Paranoia heightened. The vice grip of control and keeping the outside world at bay grew stronger.

Doctors were not to be trusted and medical intervention was seen as unnecessary. It was better to try homeopathic remedies so that doctors could be avoided. The fear of the push for vaccinations and doctors tracking patients and families for communist purposes drove most families to eschew going to a doctor for any reason. When the end of the world is near, decisions have to be made. Sometimes those decisions are life and death.

It was a strange time to be a senior in high school. At a time when I was supposed to be thinking about my future, my future felt bleak and as hopeless as a night when the moon is hidden. The light is there, it's always there. But sometimes, it's hidden from view, blocked until you unearth its presence in the tree line. Or walk farther along the forest path to better see its glimmer.

In November of 1998, my parents co-hosted a Y2K Apocalyptic Conference. There were illegal firearms and gold bars sold to prepare for a banking shutdown. Several militias were present hoping to get more men to join. Preppers were there with their canned goods and food preservation techniques. When that conference was over and the calendar turned its last page, the idea of steering clear of the world was fresh in the mind of my mom. 1999 was supposed to be the last year of life as anyone knew it. We had to live as though it were our last, preparing for the worst and never really daring to hope for the best.

That following January, I developed a cough. It progressively grew worse with passage of time. Mom would reach out to her friends that were homeopathic geniuses, one of whom was a devout Christian Scientist who believed any pharmaceuticals were not of God. I was given lots of vitamins and supplements and yet, my cough grew concerning. It became hard to breathe and my chest felt raw and crackly. About three weeks later, filled with coughing fits, sleepless nights, and more echinacea and goldenseal than I had ever had, my mom began asking around to other trusted moms who a good doctor would be to take me to, one that wouldn't require immunizations and one that wouldn't report her or track my social security number. After a few phone calls, she found a doctor that could see me.

The doctor was ancient, with his pure white hair, sparkly blue eyes, and a thousand wrinkles that told his life story on his smile lines. He was the most ineloquent doctor I have ever spoken with, and he had bizarre mannerisms. He listened to my lungs for a few minutes, wrote a prescription for amoxicillin and said, "Mom, she's got bronchitis. This will clear it up."

We filled the prescription at our local Walgreens and after weeks of being miserable, I had high hopes of being well enough to get uninterrupted sleep and to not have a nagging, croupy cough. I was able to sleep again and the hoarseness in my chest improved. It felt good to be getting better, but I didn't know what I was getting better for. The world was still ending. I panicked at night, crying, and wondering what I would be missing out on. I was grieving, thinking that college didn't matter, that I would never get married, or be able to do what I wanted to do. Growing up was my ticket out of this prison. I was worried I would be subjected to a lifetime of imprisonment based on the fear tactics I was hearing.

My rounds of antibiotics were finished in a week. My cough came back and returned with a vengeance. I told Mom I needed to return to the doctor because I didn't feel better. I was still coughing. She went and got more vitamin C and echinacea and told me that the antibiotics still needed time to work, even though I had finished them a week ago. She said not to worry, that I would get better.

But I didn't.

Slowly, I stopped eating. I had no energy and laid on the couch day after day. I took Tylenol for weeks and my mom would wrap me in hot blankets to "sweat out the fever." Dad would come home, yelling at me to stop coughing but I couldn't move. If I got up, I was lightheaded and I coughed even more. I wore a hole in the sofa. My room was too cold to sleep in.

Mom continued to take on more and more leadership roles in the homeschool group and her and Malachi were gone nearly every day. I would watch my mom and brother leave the house, knowing they wouldn't return until dinnertime. Dad would go to work. It was Whitey purring, me, and the sounds of silence all day long. On a good day, I would watch Bob Ross and paint something. I waited anxiously to have to turn the television off before my mom came into the house and discovered I had been watching it. My clothes hung on my body; my hair darkened in color. I had circles under my eyes, and I looked like a waif. It had been weeks since I'd showered, and I began to not be able to keep food down.

I began to deteriorate. Whitey would lay on my lap all day as I slept, knowing instinctively as animals do, when their owner is not well. The phone would ring, and I was too weak to pick it up to see who was calling. Mamo called nearly every day to see how I was doing, but I couldn't get to the phone all the time. Going to the bathroom, I often passed out on the floor. One time, I hit my head on the bathtub, waking up much later not remembering how I got there. I crawled back to the couch, coughing, and completely worn out.

My cough grew uncontrollable. I was vomiting blood multiple times a day, as a result of coughing chronically for weeks. I couldn't breathe. It took all of my energy to talk, so I didn't. Mamo called one night to let us know that one of my cousins was placed in a local hospital in Fairfax with pneumonia. I remembered thinking, "Why does she get to go to the hospital? I am sicker than she is." I was jealous of the care she was receiving. I wanted to feel that I mattered to someone. Mamo told my dad I needed to go to a hospital. He lied and said I was getting better.

But I wasn't.

A few nights after Mamo had called to let my dad know she saw through his incompetence; I took a turn for the worse. My breathing became all I could think about. I felt like someone much larger and heavier was sitting on my chest, preventing me from breathing all day and night. It felt like 200 pounds of pressure on my lungs. I felt smothered, crushed, and like I was drowning. I would tell myself to breathe in and out with each breath I took. As I was lying still late one night, I overheard my parent's hushed tones. They thought I was sleeping. I was really trying to stay alive.

"I really think we should take her to the hospital, Karen," dad said firmly. *Please take me, I need to go. I can't breathe.*

"I think she's fine. She's getting better. She just needs more rest. The antibiotics just need to have time to work." *I'm going to die, and no one will notice! I can't breathe, please take me to the hospital.*

"What are we going to do if we find her dead in the morning? What will we do with her body?" Dad was becoming more insistent. "Mom said Mandy is in the hospital with pneumonia. She doesn't sound good."

"She's not going to die, Richard. Don't be ridiculous."

"What are we going to do with her body if she dies?" Fear washed over me. *I'm going to die here.   Oh God! Please help me! Help them take me to the hospital!* Tones got so quiet I couldn't hear anything until finally-

"Fine," mom said in a terse, hoarse voice.   "I'll call the doctor in the morning. But we are not taking her to the hospital."

I wish I had had the skills to reach out and ask for help. It wasn't until a near decade later that I was confronted in therapy with the brutal truth that I could have saved myself if I had reached out and called   911. The harsh reality of brainwashing and living in a cult is that you aren't even aware of basic social support systems. Sure, I knew what 911 was in theory. The reality though is that I didn't think that service was available for me. I felt it was meant for others who needed help far more than I.

I was so dehydrated; the tears didn't fall anymore. I cried though somehow as my parents walked off to their bedroom at the end of the hallway. I had never felt so abandoned, worthless, and alone. I slipped in and out of consciousness that night. I had this hope of going to the doctor, but I didn't know what I would be living for. At that time, I had no friends, with no prospect of college. I was a stay-at-home-daughter destined to go from my father's house of authority to my future husband's. College was worldly, not meant for girls who were going to be homemakers. The world was ending, and I felt my life didn't have a purpose. I wanted to give up living. I wanted to die. I struggled to breathe. I was exhausted, trying to remember to take whatever labored, shallow breath I could manage. Eventually, I forgot to tell myself to breathe as exhaustion took over. I slipped into unconscious oblivion and ceased for a moment to live.

Blackness. Nothingness. Rest. Blinding light. Orange outlines, white shapes of sunburst quality. A gate. A figure in a robe, sitting on a boulder outside the gate. The hand reached for my face.

Take me home, Jesus. I want to go home. No one will care if I die. No one loves me. I can't live like this. I can't breathe. Please let me breathe again.

"Child." *Jesus, please!*

"It is not your time, yet. You are going to change the world and help other people like yourself. I know the plans I have for you. Plans to give you hope and a future. Trust me."

I startled awake, brought back to life and my harsh reality, being licked in the face by Whitey, sweating. Another massive coughing fit. I knew all I needed to do was to hold on until morning.

FREE(ISH)

My arm was draped around Mom's shoulders walking back into the doctor's office. The waiting room was very busy this Saturday morning. It was full of little kids running around, playing with activity tables, and completing puzzles. I must have looked as bad as I felt, all eyes were on me as soon as we entered. Children were staring at me, I felt so out of place, awkward. *I hate it when people stare at me.* I was struggling to breathe sitting there in the waiting room. I slumped over. I tried so hard not to cough and draw more attention to myself. It was impossible. Trying to stop the cough made it worse. Coughing made it worse. Nothing made it better. My name was called within a minute or two of being seated and we were ushered back into the room.

A new doctor arrived this time, a doctor in the practice who was younger and on call for the weekend shift. He was carrying my medical folder with him. He determined that I needed to be sent downstairs for a chest x-ray within seconds. All of the walking and moving around left me feeling like I needed to be peeled off the floor. I could barely stand. He called for a wheelchair, and I was taken to an x-ray room by a nurse. My mom followed.

"Go ahead and put your arms up over your chest," the technician requested.

I coughed. I tried to lift my arms up and they only made it halfway up my chest before I began violently coughing again.

"Try again. Arms up over your head and take a big, deep breath."

I got my arms and elbows lifted to about a 35-degree angle and then I attempted a deep breath, thinking I had somehow managed to do it completely. I fell over, coughing.

They moved me to the table. Nurses positioned my arms as my chest cavity pulled in. My arms had to be weighted down with weights to get them to stay. It wasn't much better, but they got a few rough pictures and sent them up to the doctor. The nurse came back with the wheelchair before taking me to see the doctor. I somehow managed to get out of that chair with the help of a nurse and as I got up on the table in that little room, I fought for breath. I laid down and blacked out.

"She is *very* sick!" I awoke to hear the on-call doctor shouting. *Yes, I am! Please help me!* I was fighting with everything in me to make sure that I was going to take the next breath. Talking was impossible and I was in that weird space where I was floating in and out of the blackness that would wash over me.

"No," I heard my mom say. Her voice sounded like she was speaking into a long tube, and I was on the other end of it, waiting in darkness.

"She has to get to the hospital. She can*not* go home," he said forcefully.

"I don't want to take her to the hospital," my mom said coldly, almost mechanically. *Please God! I'll die if I don't get help. Please help the doctor get me to a hospital.*

As I laid there, waiting, struggling for breath, and slipping in and out of darkness I remember thinking how I wished I could go to the hospital. I wanted to be able to breathe again and I wanted to feel worthy enough to have oxygen filling my lungs, worthy of life. The thought of having air to breathe reminded me of how good an ice-cold glass of water was on a hot summer day. I was unable to speak up or advocate for myself. Seventeen-year-old me was not asked or given the opportunity to say what I needed. My life was completely out of my hands. I had never felt so hopeless in my life.

"I'm telling you right now," Dr. LaBlonc said with laced anger, "that your daughter is very, *very* sick. She needs to get to the hospital right away."

"I do not want her to go to the hospital. We are not taking her to the hospital."

The doctor walked out of the room, seething with anger and slammed the door shut.

I opened my eyes ever so slightly as I was sitting there in the room with the one person who held my life in their hands and whom I realized never loved me. She claimed she did, but really, she loved herself. And in this instance, love was far from perfect as the love I was given was laden with fear. I glanced at my mom sitting across the room. She was stiff, stone cold, had her lips pursed and arms crossed. I wished for one small gesture of kindness or concern but there was no movement.

The doctor came back and handed my mom a piece of paper. I mustered enough strength to raise my head up to see what was going on. I still couldn't talk, but I could at least be aware, having calmed my staggered, labored breathing.

"If you don't want to take your daughter to the hospital, then I will need you to sign here. If something happens to her, this will absolve me and my practice of any responsibility." His voice was cracking. I watched, in horror and devastation as my mom signed her name on the line.

I wasn't worthy. Not worthy. That's what I saw on that line as my mom quite literally signed my life away. My life was not enough for anyone to care about. I think the doctor saw the desperation in my eyes.

"Before you can take her home, you will have to let me treat her. She needs antibiotics and some breathing treatments." Mom didn't have much choice. I was ushered into another room and was given four shots of antibiotics in my legs, steroids, and had three breathing treatments before they sent me home with a nebulizer, inhalers, steroids, and more antibiotics.

I knew when I walked in the front door of our home, that I had to leave and get out. I had a power encounter with Christ. While He didn't answer my hope to get to a hospital, I knew my life was going to be preserved by Jehovah Rapha, the God who heals. I was changed. Completely different. I walked through that door with a quiet resolve to heal, get a car, and find a way to earn my freedom. I didn't know what that looked like or what the future held. But I did know that.

It took me five months to fully recover. A little over twenty years later, I would resonate with the words of George Floyd in ways I hadn't imagined. He couldn't breathe and was robbed of his right to life and breath. I couldn't either. It humbled me realizing how little separated my life from his with those simple words. Everyone has the right to breathe.

I packed the last of my items in my car and sped off. My girlfriend and I had been given a condo to rent and friends were coming to help us move our things. *I will be free soon!* Free to live on my own. To experience the power of autonomy, choice, and voice. I thought I was going to be free. I had yet to learn that the greatest prison of all was the prison and fog that shrouded my own mind.

HOW MY BOYS SAVED ME

I remember thinking when I was 19 that I had all the answers as most typical young adults do. I had been offered a job by an angel of mercy at the church where I was attending, working in the counseling office. This was someone whom I now know was moved with compassion for me, having seen me grow up in the church we attended, being sheltered by my family. He knew I needed a job to be able to facilitate the freedom that I needed. I babysat for their grandkids and began to earn a livable wage. Working in the counseling office helped open my eyes to the hurts in my childhood. I was given free counseling as a benefit of the job and had access to an extensive counseling library. It was a balm to be heard and validated by counselors, as they listened and helped carry the pain of my childhood. I was an avid student, I read all the books housed in that counseling office and remember feeling like I had lights being turned on for the first time ever within the attic of my brain. Psychology, psychiatry, and Christian counseling had been shunned in my upbringing. To accept help, or admit one's frailty and imperfect nature, was seen as a source of shame. Having exposure to these things was new to me. I loved having new things to learn and read. It was as if these lights; these thoughts and authors were chasing away the largest shadows of my past as I dedicated myself to healing. I had become clear on what I had experienced as a child and was now comfortable labeling it abuse. I was convinced I would do things differently when the time came for me to be a mom. That time was far sooner than I had anticipated.

I will never forget when I first met him. I was 19 and he was 30. We had met at a singles group at church. We dated, became infatuated, and fought in toxic ways. Everything in our relationship happened at breakneck speed. The rush was exhilarating, exhausting, and addictive. He felt like the love my inner child wanted and needed but at the same time had also experienced; parental, controlling, dominant, authoritative love. I didn't know any other form of love, and what I knew wasn't love at all; and yet, this felt familiar. This type of affection was all I had known, and it blinded me from recognizing that when a 30-year-old man comes to try to date a 19-year-old young, naive woman that it isn't love.

Tragically, this relationship would prove to be predatory and would lead to a decade and a half of domestic violence. The physical attention was addicting, having been starved for it growing up. I thought the hours he spent talking about himself was him being vulnerable. He never asked about me unless I volunteered. Our relationship progressed until there was a night when consent wasn't given because I didn't have the words to define that then. Suddenly, at the tender age of 19, frightened, sheltered, and still a baby myself, I became pregnant and held onto that secret until I was married two months later, feeling that marrying was the only option I had.

Surprised and overwhelmed and full of shame, I was pregnant and found myself alone at 19. Two weeks after I turned 20 I was married. I felt I had no other option. If I didn't marry, I felt I would be made into a dishonored woman, having violated every law in the purity culture in which I was raised. I felt pressured by the unseen forces within my faith, family, and friend circles. I saw no other alternative. This harried decision was then followed by a baby. It was every bit as dysfunctional as the "first comes love, then comes marriage, then comes Chandra with the baby carriage" jump rope rhyme I had grown up reciting. That whole part of my life was like living in a trance-like state of mind. So, while I was free, I really wasn't. I had traded one form of bondage for another. I knew on the honeymoon when I wondered how to get an annulment and tried to look it up on the slow dial-up internet we had, that I had made a terrible mistake. Believing that love was worth fighting for and wanting to find it in all the wrong toxic places, I continued to stay.

I went through the motions of living life. I was so overwhelmed with the implications of parenting, in a toxic, abusive marriage that I began to find food as an element of comfort. I hid behind it. I lost myself in it. I denied the stress of abuse and control that continued to ravage my life. My grandma, and oddly even my mother would ask, "Are you happy?" I fought back and was adamant in defending my happiness. I was too stubborn to admit the failure of defeat, especially to my mom. When Grandma would ask though, something deep inside me was planted and eventually it made me pause and think. I was in this for life and was going to make it work, even if I had serious doubts. He was good to me some of the time and other times he was abusive. This cycle of traumatic control bonded me to him. I thought I just needed to try harder when the abuse started again, try to be something I wasn't so that the magic formula of love and acceptance would find me, like it had when we were dating. I never expected him to completely change after we were married. After all, that's what I had been taught and had reinforced growing up. Try harder, then love will find you. Be something you aren't, then you'll be accepted. I believed in my heart that I was to blame.

Within two years of marriage, I had given up everything I loved and that had made me feel alive- for him. I was isolated and berated daily. I lost myself and lost touch with the things that had made my heart sing. Things like...

My intense love of fashion and beauty, given to me by my Grammy, who taught me how to sew and inspired me to design them. *Real women don't wear makeup. Spending money on yourself is sinful,* I would hear him say to me, repeating in my head as I longingly looked through fashion magazines. My love of cats, the only living creature I had experienced comfort from as a child. *I don't like cats. If you loved me we wouldn't have them.* Going to visit my grandparents in Fairfax, the people who were my haven and refuge. *We don't have the money. If they loved you they would come down here.* My church home, the new community I had formed. *They are too liberal, too many women work. I don't like this church. We need headship theology if we are going to make this marriage work because you never learned how to submit.* Being creative, writing, the pieces that gave me confidence and joy. *No one cares about that stuff; you'll never be successful. It's embarrassing what   you   write about. I don't want you writing about me,* I would live in fear of the fights we would have if he saw me writing online. I let his censorship and control win out. When I closed the laptop screen a small piece of me died inside. Friends, the connections I was making and the people whom I wanted to spend time with and hang out with. *I don't like her. She makes you think there's something wrong with our marriage.*

I was six months pregnant with my second son when he came storming in the door, while my nine-month-old was sleeping in the other room.

"I am listing my house and we are moving." There was no discussion, just a decision issued with finality.

The weeks that proceeded were rash and moved at break-neck speed. Within a few weeks I completed a double move, seven months pregnant, alone, and found a house he said we could afford in an area 45-minutes away from the only life I had ever known. Within weeks, I was so far away, I had become effectively isolated from all of my family, friends, and church. From one form of isolation to another, I sank back into depression.

On a cold December day, where a snowstorm was forecasted I laid in a hospital bed with the headache of my life. The doctor came into my room and said that I needed blood work drawn and that my life was in critical danger. My youngest was delivered via emergency C-section hours later. He was a tiny, resilient fighter like his momma, two pounds and a few ounces more. We had been through hell and back he and I, fighting for our lives the five weeks prior to him arriving nine weeks early. Little did I know just how much our lives would change as I laid in the ICU, alone, wondering where his father was. As I drifted in and out of recovery, I knew I needed to get out of this relationship, but I had no idea how. My entire upbringing had only expected I would be a stay-at-home momma. He came on the heels of two years where my ex made an effort to make our relationship better. It quickly fell apart again during my extended hospital stay.

The day of discharge after the fight of me and my baby's life finally came and with it, brought fighting the old demons of paranoia I had been raised with. A program specializing in early intervention and therapy services, called First Steps, was wanting to qualify my tiny baby. For weeks I had been refusing to follow through with the paperwork, nurse after therapist after nurse tried encouraging and pleading with me to enroll my tiny baby in these services that were designed to help him. Still brainwashed, I felt these social workers were going to come in and look to take away my boys, report my parenting to some agency, find me abusive or any number of things that I had been told.

While placing him in the car seat for his final discharge test to go home, a nurse once more begged me to reconsider. There was something urgent in her voice, pressing me to please sign off on the paperwork of this wonderful service that my baby needed. The pleading in her voice and earnestness with which she communicated, as she took my hand in hers made me feel peacefully compelled...and I signed.

This was the impetus that began the unveiling of my cloud of paranoia and fear. This was the single incident that began the unraveling of the brainwashing I believed and what God used to untangle me and eventually set me free.

Within weeks and for the next few years, my home was filled with nurses, social workers, and therapists who did not know me personally or my background and were working tirelessly with my baby boy. Remarkably, it did not take long before I realized that the lies I had been fed about how social workers were not to be trusted were rubbish. I saw the work that they were doing, not only with my youngest but my oldest as well. I saw how dedicated these women were to help my little boys develop and grow. They were divine women who were miracle workers and angels of mercy. Frequently, I looked into the eyes of my beautiful young baby boys, and knew when I heard them giggle, or they reached out for comfort, that I had to give them more than I was handed. I knew they deserved for me to be the mom I wanted and never had. Eventually, in the space of diapering, therapy, and raising little boys, I remembered.

I remembered the conversation I had with Mamo one time, sitting at her oval shaped dining room table. We were sitting in her dining room swivel chairs that had caramel latte colored faux leather on them as I was eating Froot Loops and drinking Sunny-D, a rare treat since I was raised on bulgur wheat and bran muffins.

"What do you want to do when you graduate high school, Chandra?"

"I don't know," I swirled my cereal around with my spoon. "I really want to be a stay-at-home mom. I think I would like to be an interior designer because then I can use my skills to help my family someday."

"Oh, that's nice. That's real nice." She got quiet as she watched me pour another bowl. "Have you ever thought about being a teacher? I think you'd be really good at it."

My bright, blue eyes peered up over the top of my mound of Froot Loops on my spoon and our eyes met. Mine, locked on her royal blue ones. At that moment I didn't know what my future held but it was as if Mamo was holding back a curtain to a life I hadn't previously seen, showing me an option, I hadn't considered for myself. Mamo provided a glimmer of hope into the future.

And as I remembered that hopeful seed that had laid dormant all those years, I realized that it was not too late to begin something new. I knew I needed to make a change and even though I was scared, I knew I would need to be able to provide for myself. I knew I would need to provide for myself in some capacity because my boys deserved a peaceful home. A few weeks later, I walked through the doors of school for the very first time in my life. If it hadn't been for my high-risk pregnancy and premature delivery, if it hadn't been for those nurses who knew that early intervention services were needed, if it hadn't been for God placing just the right social service workers in my life, my life would have looked very different. I wouldn't have remembered.

I sat in the advisor's office, anxiously awaiting my appointment time. Everyone, much younger than me, seemed so confident and self-assured. I was nothing short of paralyzed. This felt so completely foreign to me, to be in an institution I had been raised to fear. I knew what I was doing was brave though. No less brave than having faced death in the face two times.

With the knowledge that I was strong (but had yet to really discover and believe how truly strong I was), I pushed back the voices inside me that told me I was going to fail.

"Ms. Hawkins?" a voice called.

An hour later, I had a plan put together by a patient advisor who outlined everything I would need in order to get started on this next chapter in my life. I left, empowered. All I could see when my mind was reeling with information overload...*Do you have a FAFSA? What about a Pell Grant? What high school did you go to? What courses did you take?*...were the faces of my three little boys whom I knew would need me to do whatever I could to ensure they had an example to follow. I wanted them to see their mom push herself to new limits, to be the first woman in her immediate family to finish a college degree. I wanted to give them a better life. I pushed back the voices of accusation and shame that I wouldn't be successful, and I forged forward and kept answering Susan's questions, clear on my immediate purpose.

They didn't know it then, but in that moment, my boys saved me. It was their little souls and sweet smiles that I held to my heart. They deserved better. I knew I did too.

WARFARE

For me, even the consideration of teaching in a public school with my upbringing felt like the ultimate form of being Public Enemy Number One. I was taught to fear and mistrust systems and structures where accountability and people outside The Remnant congregated. I was taught that the classrooms across America were daily filling children's minds with brainwashing. This was similar to the angry harbingers of today. People assume that our students are taught by liberal teachers who are pushing the ominous, vague "agenda" of the left; indoctrinating impressionable young minds in the theories of socialism, critical race theory, communism, and evolution, empowered by the government. I was engulfed in the belief that public schools were tools used by Satan and as I grew up I came to feel that should I step foot in one that I would somehow be contaminated, in danger of eternal damnation. Cutting through the shrouds of mental torment, while fighting through the darkness of feeling like I was condemned to hell was difficult to say the least.

Homeschooling, at its inception, was a reaction of the religious right wanting to provide an educational alternative to the secular psychological theories that were emerging from the 1960's and 70's. It began at first as an educational movement by John Holt and a little later by authors Raymond and Dorothy Moore, educational progressives who were recognizing that the one-size-fits-all approach of public education in the 1970's was not serving all kids. Their desire was to draw attention to the downfalls of the current approaches in public education and to give families, whose kids were not excelling, a high-quality alternative to education. This alternative recognized that a one-size-fits-all approach works about as well as assigning the same training regimen for professional athletes. It doesn't always work. The "unschooling" approaches of Holt and the Moore's were popularized by the religious right's desire to keep their children protected from what they deemed to be harmful cultural theories from the Sexual Revolution and the Civil Rights Movement. Theories, they feared, were making their way into American classrooms.

As the religious right and their fears of government intrusion grew, so grew their interest in the idea of keeping children unstained by the world- through homeschooling and parochial schools, cultivating a socially isolated, homogenous bubble. The antagonism towards the public school system by homeschoolers began in the 1980's as the culture-war Baby Boomers began to raise their kids. Many new homeschoolers came from the free love progressive movement of the 1960's and 1970's, who had found religion. Namely, Christian legalism, steeped like a Boston teabag in rules and the confines of how one is to behave in this world. Homeschooling gained traction through James Dobson when he became an outspoken supporter of the concept of homeschooling through his organization, Focus on the Family. Homeschooling has continued to grow to become an option for middle-class, blue-collar families who have felt they do not have the means to send their kids to private school and desire an alternative to traditional public schooling. "Training up a child," has become the *modus operandi*, a way to ensure carbon copies of this idyllically disillusioned religion.

When a group internalizes their perceived superiority over another group, harsh judgements emerge. Whether vocalized or not, these seeds took root within my family and others around me. To engage with (to borrow a phrase from the television show *Lost*), The Others, suddenly becomes a threat. As a superior person, you've constructed in your mind this perfect world, a world unstained by others. A world that you've built in response to what you fear. When confronted (whether overtly or covertly) with what you fear, it threatens the very foundation of what you believe and have built your reality upon. These feelings have the power to make you uneasy and distrustful, and in my experience, combative and hateful.

Engaging with a different worldview threatens the lens in which you view it when insecurity reigns. This contributes to and creates polarized people groups. The combativeness and antagonism create the culture wars we find ourselves in today where people scream at one another in the drop-off line and at school board meetings. It submerges dialogue and encourages blanket statements and stereotypes. It encourages people to spew harassment and verbal abuse on the internet, and God knows what else around the Thanksgiving table.

The culture war that I was raised in is as tragically familiar as these polarized Facebook wars that we see daily on our social media feeds and during our polarizing Presidential elections. I was raised to believe that to engage with, partner with, or even participate in group sports, proms, or visits within a public-school setting would somehow cause me to lose my salvation, that partnership with such institutions would somehow weaken my faith and cause me to lose my way. These rites of high school passage were thought to be an evil influence. Partnering with the pervasively evil public school system meant being worldly. Being "of this world" was something to fear and avoid at all costs. It came from the misrepresentation and misinterpretation of the Apostle Paul's letter to the early Roman church. A favorite passage we were required to memorize was found in Romans 12:1-2, *(ESV)*:

"I appeal to you therefore, brothers, by the mercies of God, to present your bodies as a living sacrifice, holy and acceptable to God, which is your spiritual worship. Do not be conformed to this world, but be transformed by the renewal of your mind, that by testing you may discern what is the will of God, what is good and acceptable and perfect."

Being free from "the world" meant staying holy and in order to be holy, we had to stay away from worldliness. This term, practically applied to my young life, meant staying away from anything that was trendy, culturally in sync, or mainstream in order to attain the ideal of holiness. The application was rigid, intolerant, and judgmental of others. It meant the practice of legalistic behaviors that kept those who did not look, act, or believe as we did at arm's length. It was a failure to apply the second half of this passage and was instead, a willful attempt to do the exact opposite, choosing to intentionally live with a Pharisaical attitude:

> *"God has given me grace to speak a warning about pride. I would ask each of you to be emptied of self-promotion and not create a false image of your importance."*
> *Romans 12:3, The Passion Translation*

Devastatingly, the seeds of hatred and intolerance that were sown during the culture wars of the 1980 and 90's towards those that were different from us. These seeds have taken full-blown root. The Church once again missed the opportunity to confront this in their pulpits. The Christian church in America has missed decades of opportunities to confront the horrors of slavery, abuse, and domestic violence so the absence of confronting culture wars and judgementalism should not be shocking. I clearly remember the pastors that knew we were legalistic and judgmental. I knew who saw the sadness behind my longing eyes. They knew that I wasn't allowed to go to age-segregated Sunday school or youth group, yet these pastors never confronted these attitudes from the pulpit or behind closed doors to my parents. They didn't want to offend them and cause my parents to leave. My parents, and others like them, believed in sacrificial giving and regularly tithed their ten percent to the local church.

And yet. Two decades have gone by and the divisions remain intense within our country. These divisions are pervasive. I wonder if perhaps these divisions would have been addressed that the smaller streams, like legalism in what a woman wears or a family's school choice, might have been forged. These smaller channels are now chasms and Grand Canyons within America. Public schools are still the enemy and teachers remain the villains. Christians are still fighting one another over science and evolutionary concepts, they continue to war against the humanity of people of color and the right for marginalized people to have a voice. Women are still told what to wear and what type of healthcare they should have. Association with those who act or believe differently than us is seen as a threat and staying in a socially isolated bubble has become an intentional decision. We can easily create this bubble through deliberate choice in whom we interact with on social media. C.S. Lewis stated it best, *"The essential vice, the utmost evil, is pride..."* Sadly, this is where we are right now. No one is listening against the cacophony of voices swirling in our heads. We fail to see one another as Jesus saw us, and we have missed the mark as the Church on how to build bridges over the chasms that divide us.

Within this bizarre intersectionality where my underlining privileges allowed my parents to homeschool, where my connection and relationship to the systems that had completely failed me, where my resilience and rebellion against what I was being taught was stronger than my obedience to the group think and hatred I was subjected to; it was here in this intersection of my life that I found myself pushing back on the brainwashing and wanting to push past the lies to what I had been taught about those that were different than me. I found myself stepping inside these public schools, these "Satanic houses of worship" (as my mom called them), ready to wage war on all the lies I had been taught.

My great-grandpa, or Grampy as I affectionately called him, was the athletic director and high school basketball and football coach in Fairfax. He brought home several state championships, taught Spanish, and was loved by all for the twinkle in his eye and the way he slapped his knee when he laughed. He was bilingual before it was cool, and proud of his Cherokee heritage. His granddaughter was first a teacher in that same school, later a principal and eventually went on to earn her doctorate. My mom's family prized public education so when my mom decided she was going to homeschool me, and announced it to the family, there was a family feud that erupted, only Steve Harvey wasn't moderating. Visiting for holidays was clouded in family drama, started by my mom who would try to argue her point of view in order to gain approval, hoping that her family would validate her choices. I clearly remember the fight my mom had with her parents over their concerns for the way I was being raised.

"We are worried about the kids," Grandma said, anxiety and concern lacing her hoarse voice.

"You don't need to be worried about them, Mom. They are *fine*." Mom's iciness stood in contrast to Grandma's unique, warm raspiness. I was listening on the stairway that went upstairs. The door to the kitchen was cracked and I sat on the fifth stair from the bottom, making sure to skip the super squeaky one.

Grandpa chimed in. "Karen, you don't get it. You have those kids involved in a cult!" His black coffee mug clanked down hard on the kitchen table; I pictured his tar black coffee sloshing over the side as it hit with a loud smack.

Several rounds, more heated than the first, went on. Mom, defensive, denying, accusing. Grandma worried, anxious, wanting a solution. Grandpa, angry. Angry at Mom and angry at his inability to change her stubborn mind and protect his grandkids. I felt validated for the first time. It was a comforting feeling to know that I had an adult who saw the crazy in my life. It was Grandpa's care and honest comment that became the impetus I would need to process my experiences through an alternate perspective and what I would need to hear in my mind to set myself free. I needed to hear I was raised in a cult, because it was truly the only way to process what I was living.

Cult members do not want to hear they are involved in one or that they believe lies that are harmful to their families. Cults exist on the premise of false dichotomies and lies. Cult members are cemented to these falsehoods by buying the deception that the cult has the corner market on truth. We left Grandma and Grandpa's house abruptly and Mom forbade us from spending the night at their home for years to come. The culture war wasn't only being fought in grassroots politics, cold calling, and the newsrooms across America. The culture war was happening in my own family, around the dining room table and over my Grandma's made with love meals.

Into young adulthood I emerged, deeply conflicted over whether public schools were as Satanic as I had been trained to believe. Mamo's students would come back and find her, decades later, thanking her for her impact on their lives. They talked of her creativity, of her ability to help them learn to read and to know their multiplication tables. When I found her college textbooks and Grade Teacher magazines from the 1940's, her penciled annotations and delicate, yellow clippings of projects whispered of her teaching process and love of her students and craft.

Grampy was wickedly clever and kind. He was legendary, a hero of Fairfax. It wasn't just because of his coaching and teaching, it spanned beyond that. It was his passion for teaching and helping others grow, inspiring others to achieve that fueled the admiration of an entire town. My aunt followed suit. Loved and adored by all because she was Marvin's granddaughter. Her confidence, her poise, her passion to turn failing impoverished schools around was contagious.

And yet, I was taught to fear the glass doors and brick walls. I was taught that Satan was active and alive, fighting some ominous spiritual battle to build his army for Armageddon. Slowly, I began to challenge my presuppositions and brainwashing, beginning with that first faint crack of realization: Mamo and Grampy weren't agents of evil, part of some sinister plan. They were my grandparents and they loved me. I realized they loved people and that they had both made tremendous impacts on those around them. As I aged, I realized the only warfare that existed was the one that was man made and completely one-sided, typically taking place around controversial family dinners and antagonistic, spirited debates, fueled by fear, sin, and selfishness.

Teaching, and Mamo's desire for me to be a part of it, inspired me to see within myself something that no one else had unlocked.

FIRST DAYS OF SCHOOL

"The most important day of a person's education is the first day of school, not graduation day."
-Harry Wong, <u>The First Days of School</u>

I was entering my final semester of student teaching in August of 2014. Schools came to a screeching halt and called off students and teachers attending as protests emerged among St. Louis, filling up the streets. Michael Brown had been tragically murdered just a week before students were to be in session. He was murdered on the same street I grew up playing on. Things had truly come full circle and this complex multi-intersectionality continued to play out in my life.

Systemic injustice and segregation run deeper than the Mississippi River in St. Louis. The city appears to be caught between the desires for progression and the deep-set loyalty to industrialism. Protestors sought to upend this paradoxical intersection. The riots that sprang up were, as Dr. Martin Luther King, Jr. said, "The voice of the unheard." Businesses were boarded up and some were destroyed. Schools were closed as student-led protests sprang up. Racial tension was thicker than the humidity. You could feel the tide of racism ebb and flow from zip code to zip code within the metro area.

Living in a white, segregated, middle-class area my boys were unaffected in their school. I was just beginning to see and witness what my friends had seen, experienced, and lived their entire lives. I did what was the first step in unshackling my privileged lens. I sat, I listened, I waited, I watched, and I shut my mouth for the next year. I learned about the issues surrounding systemic injustice and racism that I had previously refused to see. I educated myself on the issues of inequity in St. Louis, in particular, educational inequities. The more I absorbed the more this cause resonated with me on a deeply personal level. In some strange way, these two worlds: cultic, fundamentalist homeschooling and systemic injustice, were colliding into an intersection. An intersection where two vastly different worlds collided with a mutual understanding that when systems fail; they fail children, they fail families, and they fail our collective whole.

I'll never forget the overwhelming feeling of humility and responsibility I felt as I found out that I had finally been granted the privilege of a classroom of my own. The tug I felt on my heart was to go "urban." When God calls, He sends and equips, does He not? I had no idea what I was about to learn, the ways He was going to open my eyes, or the ways that He was going to use me to transform these young scholar's lives. Young, green, and fresh out of college I landed that first-grade classroom after an extensive interviewing process. all asked of a teacher who was fresh out of college not asking to make more than forty thousand a year.

God placed me in this classroom, in this school, with these amazing professionals for such a time as this. In one of the most segregated schools in the nation, along what is known as the Delmar Divide.

I had suffered such educational neglect that the strongest value I brought with me was the idea that education is a right and not a privilege of every child in America. As I prepared my classroom, alone, having no idea what I was doing in any real sense, I began to trust my intuition. Doing what I knew in my heart was right for my students, the children that became like my own for a year.

They don't teach you these things in college. I was preparing for my open house with stations and cute, colorfully printed signs. I prepared a PowerPoint presentation that highlighted who I was and included my philosophy on how students learn. Late into the night, I worked on assembling the goodie bags I made for my first graders. It didn't matter that I was using my own money. I was called.

With the open house setup completed after long hours and many late nights decorating my classroom, the open house was upon me. I was instantly humbled. Only one other family represented my skin color. The moment that fact dawned on me, I felt such inadequacy. *Maybe I won't be what my students need! What if I fail them?* And then, in that same moment that the doubt began to swirl, the parents were all seated, and I had no other choice but to keep moving forward. That's the thing with schools that I had yet to realize, the system moves at a breakneck pace with hardly enough time to reflect. Teachers and students are thrown into this rapid current, together, and before you know it just one minute, one subject, one hour, one day, one quarter becomes summer. Time does not stand still or halt in a time warp, as much as teachers wish it would.

My first open house began with parents bringing their first graders with them. I was struck how involved the parents were, so concerned about their child's well-being. Every one of my students had on the whitest of kicks, beautifully done hair, and freshly ironed shirts. These families wanted their children to know the value they placed on education; how vital it was to their success in life. These families- my families- came in and offered me the respect they placed on the title of a teacher. I commanded their full attention for the next hour or so as I outlined who I was and answered their questions. There was one moment in particular where I explained that my method of teaching was not to sit down and complete a worksheet, but to have students learn through transformational, innovative, hands-on learning.

My eyes locked with the eyes of the parents of my students, and I could feel the entire room breathe a sigh of relief. This was the first incident where I knew my gut instinct was correct and I listened to it. After years of doubting what I felt and being told what to think and how to feel, this was monumental. Being able to channel my intuition and listen to it gave me confidence to do it again. These beautiful, respectful, caring parents gave me the courage to listen to myself in that tiny moment. A moment which appeared inconsequential was the first of many pebbles I would learn to lay down, creating the foundation of listening to myself and doing what my students, and ultimately, what myself needed.

For far too long, schools in impoverished, urban areas rely on the industrial era approach to education where students are asked to "sit and get." Instead of realizing that students need to be curators, innovators, and dispellers of their own, often harsh realities, we keep them segregated, confined. Expecting that if we teach the skills that facilitate lower wage-earning jobs such as filling out paperwork and precious little innovation, that this will somehow help enable students to rise above the shadows and confines of poverty doing innovative tasks alongside Elon Musk and Steve Jobs. We expect to see different results yet use the same methods we have been using since the New England Primer was introduced in Plymouth.

Schools with access to resources, conversely in wealthy, typically white-presenting areas are afforded the opportunities for innovative education. The changes to fighting the system and structure of the bureaucracy of education are formidable because these schools have access to resources that schools in impoverished areas do not. Resources such as money for professional development, support from parent teacher organizations due to higher percentage of stay-at-home parents, teachers that aren't stressed over high stakes testing because these students typically perform better on standardized tests, and schools that aren't afraid of losing accreditation because their students traditionally score higher on standardized tests. These factors matter because the children in the poor, marginalized school districts that are struggling to maintain accreditation have a right to an education that is innovative, creative, and transformative. Even more so as they deserve to have an education that helps them rise above the trauma of poverty, and institutional and structural racism. It isn't possible without resources.

I knew I had to be a mold changer, a shape shifter and after that first night, I knew in my heart of hearts that my students deserved everything that I brought to the table, and so much more. They deserved someone who would take bold risks to give them the best start in their life, a teacher who could teach them to read that would prevent years of reading intervention. Intervention that would keep them out of the classroom, away from valuable content that is taught. My students deserved an advocate. I knew that I had to be that transformative teacher, that teacher that shielded my students from the pressures of administration and fear of a pink slip at the end of the year. They had the right to an amazing education, just as I did, and wished that I had had- and didn't.

I was confident that God had placed me in this classroom, with these families, for such a time as this. I was confident of my calling and that I was exactly what my first graders needed. I had no idea how heavy some of their stories would become. Nor how much I would in turn become transformed.

After the supplies that had been dropped off had been put away and organized, after the percentage of parent attendance had been calculated from Open House, and student name tags placed on desks, the first day of school was upon me. Cans of Play-doh were at each desk. Back to school read-alouds were displayed on the bookshelf. I was proud of the vision I had thus far achieved.

Rainbow borders were stacked and layered creating colorful bulletin boards. Inviting books were placed on display. Puppets and blocks were prominent, subtly showing that I intended to guard playtime for my first graders. Alphabet cards in rainbow colors with chalkboard font were placed on the massive bulletin board. I intended to use this as my word wall to help my students with vocabulary acquisition. A rocking chair for morning meetings and where we would read aloud and learn together was next to the easel and objective board. The six computers were stationed against the wall. Wicker baskets held crayons, colored pencils, erasers, pencil grips, and fidgets for little people who had strong emotions. Rainbow ribbons were tied to branches to create interest and spark joy. All that was needed were the little people who were going to learn here.

I looked at their names on my roster and placed removable name tags at each desk. Romero. Anthony. Nadia. Zahra. Ryan. Jerome. Megan. Traydon. Shay. Candy. Darrius. Jazmine. Akeem. Lila. Drew. Soon they filed in and began to work with the Play-Doh at their desk, following the prompt to "make your favorite toy." It was the smallest class in years in this building.

As the last parent left, nearly forty minutes after school started, I took a minute to soak in this moment before I shut my classroom door. This moment, where I surveyed my Sparkling Scholars. Here they were, happy and giggling. It was up to me to ensure we could become a family and that I could teach them all the things they would need in first grade to be successful later. It was up to me to hold their souls and hearts, to guide and direct them. They were given to me for a year to teach, but they taught me so much more.

A G(RACE)FUL
TRANSFORMATION

The first few months of teaching my Sparkling Scholars were behind me. I had navigated the first few days of school with relative ease and was smart enough to know I needed to listen to my heart and yet be humble enough to ask for ideas and help. I received positive praise and feedback from my principal and literacy coaches.

One of the most impactful insights I had from my principal was after a walk through that she did.

"Every time I come into your room I breathe a sigh of relief. Whenever I need a break, I go and sit in your room and am so thankful. I don't have to worry about anything." She collapsed into the rocking chair in my room until her walkie-talkie prompted her to leave. I knew that I was doing a good job of knitting these little people into a family, some of them the only family they experienced. I knew that I needed to have high expectations so that the gaps they had from kindergarten didn't impact them later.

Several of my kindergarteners that came to me were from an ineffective teacher's classroom the year before. A white teacher, teaching in a nearly all-black school. Her bias towards students who were not from a cultural lens she could relate to enabled her to make decisions where these babies were allowed to spin around in circles on the floor, cry in a corner, and simply refuse to learn to read because it was hard for them. This teacher failed to understand the struggles that would impact these students. While this teacher did lack administrative support, the excuse is invalid. Teachers are more often than not thrown into a classroom, with little oversight except on occasion where a coach or principal gives us feedback on a thirty-minute window of our day. Teachers are expected to address the needs, to do it well, and do it with minimal issues or guidance. Some do it better than others. Some have more giftedness and "with-it-ness" than others. In education there is a phrase that is often said in interview panels of new teacher hires. "It's the 'it' factor. You either have it or you don't."

Some of these teachers let their racism and bias cloud their judgment and only focus on the kids that talk, walk, and live lives similar to their own, often blinded to their own prejudice.

Though I had much to learn about my students and their struggles, and a lot that I had not yet been awoken to in terms of white privilege, being true to myself was exactly what my students needed. I knew that they deserved a teacher who showed up and gave 100% of her personal best every day. I knew that they deserved someone who had high expectations so that they could learn what was needed and required. I knew that they needed love, empathy, consistency, no excuses, and that they deserved and had a right to an excellent education. I knew that my Sparkling Scholars deserved the opportunity to learn. Rita Pierson helped solidify my philosophy with her now famous Ted Talk before I ever met my little students. It was when she said, "Every child deserves a champion: an adult who will never give up on them, who understands the power of connection and insists they become the best they can possibly be," that I knew what my purpose was because the song in my own heart was confirmed through her work. My own inner child needed a champion, someone who understood the power of connection. So, I sought to be that for the kids who needed a champion, the forgotten ones on the other side of the Delmar Divide.

In this unlikely intersection where a white teacher, coming from a poor yet privileged and racist background who as a young girl watched a system fail her and wished that she had one teacher or advocate in her life that saw her struggle and helped her rise above, and where poor, middle class black children saw and experienced things that no one should have to see or experience and had the option of not learning to read because your kindergarten teacher didn't want to invest in you; in this weird intersection, I became their champion because I knew what it felt like to not have one. I gave them a safe space that they hated leaving at the end of the day. There were often tears at the end of the day. They taught me about their worlds, the values of their families, and ingrained in my heart that their lives, and the lives of their entire families and communities, mattered. Together, we became a family.

October. The month where countless professional development days are held, additional responsibilities are asked of teachers, the curriculum gets kicked into high gear, and the month of parent teacher conferences.

When families have a freak out moment, it is going to be in October. It's the month of newly sharpened pencils, pumpkins, and parents. It was also the month of awakening for me.

I'll never forget that moment the shackles fell off my feet and I began dancing in the streets, fully awake. That moment I realized that everything I had been taught to fear was a lie. The moment when family after family came into parent teacher conferences with me and we switched roles. I, the student, my families, the teachers.

Anthony's dad sat across the table from me. This same man had I seen him three years prior, I would have clutched my purse harder, clung to the wall tighter, and gave a fearful glance making my obvious discomfort and racist beliefs known. I would have crossed the street and had my hand on my cell phone. This father, in that moment sitting across from me in my classroom, did more for me than he will likely ever know.

He had a grill that gleamed and glittered and the color of being a Blood that was prominently displayed in his choice of clothing. His eyes, though narrow, twinkled. He was the exact stereotype of a man I had been actively taught to judge in haste.

"Hello, ma'am. How are you?" Anthony's dad pulled up a seat, making eye contact with me. We exchanged smiles. His respectful, gentle manner confronted my schema, and I had no choice but to create a new file folder in my mental filing cabinet to place my now new perspective.

For the next half hour Anthony's dad and I met together on my Damascus road, two worlds apart coming together for one purpose: to ensure that his son and my scholar had the best possible outcome in first grade. I acknowledged how kind, thoughtful, respectful, and gifted his youngest son was. I was especially impressed by Anthony's work ethic in first grade and how much pride he took in his work. Anthony's dad and I exchanged laughs over his son's antics. I shared with him one particular story that highlighted how much of an impact Anthony's Granny had had on him. A story which I knew could get me in trouble teaching in a public school, but Anthony's family understood my heart. Sometimes ministry for Jesus takes precedence over the fear that we harbor. Granny knew the importance of helping to secure good outcomes in a world that is terrifying and unpredictable for young, black boys. One way to do this was to raise them going to church on Sunday. Her life motto was found in the words of Ye, "Raise our sons, train them in the faith."

I recounted the vignette for Anthony's dad.

"One day, right before art class, Anthony was having a lot of trouble following my directions and was making weak choices, being influenced by his friend who was also struggling."

"Oh no, Ms. Hawkins, we can't be havin' him not followin' your directions," he said with concern.

I laughed. "I agree, but I don't think it will be much of an issue anymore because I think I got through to him." He nodded.

I continued. "I pulled Anthony out of line after everyone else had gone into art and asked him, 'Who are you hurting right now by not following our class expectations?'"

Anthony shrugged. I asked the question again, getting closer to his eye level.

His eyes started to tear up as I gave him some time to think before pressing for an answer. I had my teacher gaze on him. His voice quivered.

"Granny?" He said hesitantly.

I masked a giggle. "Yes, you are upsetting her, but there's someone else you are upsetting."

"Who?" I pointed my finger toward heaven. There was a long pause.

"God?"

"Yes. He wants you to do what is right and He knows you can." I shared with Anthony's dad that he was golden the rest of the day as we chuckled over the fact that all I had to do was point to the heavens any time he started clowning around from there on out.

It was obvious Anthony's dad had a passion in his heart for his young sons. He wanted better for them. He was fighting for their future, in this very moment, in what felt like a sacred space as my own racial lens melted and a transformation took place in my heart. Anthony's dad had just gotten out of serving jail time. Jail time, I later found out, for being one of the individuals who started the riots after Michael Brown's murder. A man whom the news wanted to vilify, was the same man who in an instant taught me more about racism than countless books ever could.

At that moment, in that space, I was the student in my classroom. My fear melted and with it, the shreds of racism. My eyes were opened, like Paul's were on the road to Damascus when the blinding light of transformation helped him to see. To see how vital it is to question those beliefs you've been taught as a child. To recognize that fear lies to you, whispering seeds of doubt and mistrust. When we are taught to fear people of color and avoid spaces where diversity and ethnicities mingle, this breeds mistrust. It encourages judging a person on outward appearances, and this directly contradicts what God tells us in 1 Samuel 16:7b, *"For the Lord sees not as man sees: man looks on the outward appearance, but the Lord looks on the heart."*

My teacher was the black man that America and my parents had actively taught me to fear and hate. He melted my heart and as my circle widened, I saw the lies, the mirror dimly lit became clear, and fear was erased. Everything I had been taught as a child in that space of thirty minutes was dissolved into shatters as my blind eyes saw. Just as quickly as Paul who had *"something like scales fall from his eyes,"* (Acts 9:18, MSG) on his Damascus Road; my own eyes were opened as the Holy Spirit whispered conviction to my heart. Fear lies, but love listens.

#COLORBRAVE

My circle grew wider the next day as I met with Akeem's family for the second day of parent teacher conferences.

His mom was soft spoken. She was gentle, kind, and sweet. He and his sisters were equally so. Bright, sparkly, brown eyed people who had laughter that sounded like a bubbling brook, happily splashing over rocks. I could only guess at the color of the girls' hair, as it was covered with beautiful Hijabs daily. No doubt it was similar to Akeem's large espresso-colored curls. His dad was fighting in the civil war over in Yemen, so his uncle came to his conference filling in as the head of the family.

I had known his background from the beginning.

This little guy hated school. On the Developmental Reading Assessment (DRA) which levels scholars' reading abilities from A (beginning reader) to Z (advanced reader), he didn't earn a placement score from kindergarten. His native language was Arabic, and he did not engage with his peers. Often sullen, he struggled, and joy was absent from his countenance.

The only and eldest son of a devout Sunni family, the pressure to learn was tremendous for him. His mom frequently worried about his English-speaking abilities and reading progress, and she needed frequent updates on his progress. I knew that Akeem needed joy, acceptance, and encouragement. His grandparents, living in Dearborn, MI had even kept Akeem out of school for a time during kindergarten as he hated it so much. His Grandpa spent time with him, hoping to help Akeem learn English. Frustrated at his lack of progress, he was placed back into the public school I now taught.

A Sunni Muslim family, a father fighting in a Yemenis civil war, grandparents living in Dearborn, MI, and a little boy who hated school were factors that my Judeo-Conservative upbringing would have wanted me to place in a box and make a judgement call about.

It was hard to hear the rhetoric at home from my then-husband. Hatred for Muslims and calls for deportation from my ex were a constant drip. I was fighting for my own freedom. I risked facing yelling, shame, and emotional abuse should I challenge this thinking and that wasn't something I could endure. When I would try to confront his thinking, I was told how "stupid," "ignorant," and "wrong" I was. His circle was narrow, and his mind narrower still. As my circle widened, so did my thinking. I was becoming color brave.

It became painful, hearing him belittle people made in God's image. Beautiful people whom I now fully understood their dignity and humanity, no longer a news story and scripted rhetoric or Fox News feature. I felt a powerful connection to these souls. They had changed my heart and my love for this family grew as I saw the impact I was having on Akeem.

I always loved a challenge. I knew this little scholar had a capacity to learn and was easily discouraged and needed specific feedback and praise. He needed a teacher who saw him as he was and that could encourage the effort he was making. Throughout the course of those first few weeks, I took bold risks. I incorporated puppetry into a center choice. I believed it would help my kids with language and social skills development. I integrated as much play as I could. Playing, I felt, was something that was non-negotiable and play, to me, was sacred.

Playing for me when I was a child was my safe space. It sheltered me from the trauma of my home. No one interrupted my world and within my imagination no one intruded. Play was a crucial part of the resilience I was able to foster within myself because in those imaginary worlds, hope existed. I could envision a life that was different than the one I had. It helped me rise above. Being able to play was an undeniable blessing and benefit to my homeschool education and one that I wouldn't change. I brought that value with me now, into a structured classroom setting.

Coming into my own classroom I knew the statistics. One in four of my little people were likely facing abuse and trauma. Using play as a sacred space for my scholars to express feelings, engage in social skills, and envision a life better than the one they had was critical to my classroom management. I didn't care what I was being asked to teach, I was absolutely going to guard the sacred space of play in my room.

Every center was play-based and tied to a state learning standard. I believed that through play, my scholars were still learning, constructing meaning into their worlds through play. Choices included puppets, blocks, writing and art, kitchen, and dramatic play.

Within these choices my sparkling scholars thrived. I worked hard to ensure what I did was backed by standards and then tuned out all the other voices. Including my skeptical teammates.

I watched as play therapists, special educators, administrators, and school counselors marveled at my ability to help struggling students, non-verbal students, shy and socially challenged students succeed and grow by unspeakable bounds. Akeem was one of my biggest success stories.

As my scholars began to envelop him in their world of play, Akeem made friends. He began to laugh. Slowly, he began using words and by December he was speaking in full sentences. Every moment I saw an attempt at speaking a new word or attempting a new skill, I instantly offered praise. How his sparkling brown eyes gleamed and his icy exterior melted when I let him know he was applying the right strategy when trying to read. He thrived.

When I was in college full-time, I began substitute teaching. I worked in an early childhood center for an urban district that has since become nationally recognized. It was here that my introduction into urban educational practices began.

I'll never forget her. She was the school counselor for the Early Childhood Center where I had been substituting. With skin the color of perfect caramel, she confidently rocked her gorgeous natural hair before natural hair was widely accepted, had a voice that was calming to triggered little people and anxious adults, and a laughter that was infectious. In education all educators are the sum total of those who have walked before us, those that have shared with us, and taught us what they know. I have been the recipient of greatness in my career and Denise was great.

Through her and my time at the ECC, I learned how little people need to be spoken to. I learned that little people need advocates, and they need to learn how to use their voices. As a traumatized adult child, my inner child began to heal as a result of watching her be an agent of healing in that school. She and I would talk often about what children needed in and out of the classroom, she shared her books and resources with me.

The most pivotal component she taught me was how to be color brave. We were sitting in her office discussing a challenging student and his needs. I was the staff assigned to work primarily with him and while he was traumatized and triggered easily, Denise gracefully challenged me and my presuppositions.

"What he needs is for people to not see him as though they are color blind. He needs people to be color brave," she gently challenged me.

Curious, I asked. "What does it mean for people to be color brave?"

Denise smiled. She knew if I was serious about learning, I'd follow through. "Look it up on TedTalks. It means to see people as they really are and to refuse to not see the color of their skin. To recognize that our experiences are different."

She observed the confused look on my face.

"We all want to be seen for who we are. When people are color blind they say they don't see the color of our skin. That's not what is needed. We need more people to be color brave, to see us as we really are."

She sent me the link to the TedTalk, and I listened. My eyes were opening, my mind was becoming aware, my heart growing in empathy and understanding. Listening to Mellody Hobson's TedTalk, *Color Blind or Color Brave?*, in the aftermath of what had happened in Ferguson just months prior was a critical part of my journey into a woke reality. The discussions of systematic injustice and white privilege in mainstream culture had just begun and I was enlightened.

I began to ask myself daily, *How can I be color brave today?* It was this very question and subsequent goal that I had, to be color brave, that helped me navigate the waters of avoiding premature judgment calls towards those who were different than myself. The daily decision of being color brave helped me to push   aside   the political rhetoric that my ex would bring home and play in the background on the nightly news. It protected my heart from being calloused and assigning racist stereotypes to a sweet family who was worried about their struggling son. As I began to cultivate a color brave classroom community, I took risks. I knew that to ensure all voices, souls, and families were honored in my classroom I would need to be inclusive. I began to make decisions that were true to what I believed my Sparkling Scholars needed. Creating a color brave classroom wasn't a topic that was being written about much in education at the time, but I knew that there were other teachers whose souls were tied to mine, doing the same hard and holy work of integrating inclusive racial practices in their own classrooms. We were fueled by the protests taking place in high schools across America due to the racial divide highlighted by the murder of Michael Brown. I looked through my classroom library and got rid of titles that were based on Christian Nationalism and inaccurate historical perspectives. This was a bigger step to my own recovery than I realized. So many titles that I had previously purchased were books that I was raised to believe were good literature for children. Every time I sorted through a title that I threw away (I refused to hand them out) I shook my head and shuddered. I made intentional purchases of books that featured the voices and stories of people of color. I displayed them prominently in my classroom. Black History was not just a month-long focus in February. I special ordered multicultural skin tone crayons and markers so my students could draw themselves accurately. Dolls were placed on shelves that reflected the beautiful brown skin of the little girls and boys in my room. And slowly, my room began to reflect the children I served. The unique holidays that my Sparkling Scholars celebrated became a ritual where they could share with us about their family traditions and customs.

It was within this corrected framework, this corrected prescription of my vision, that I became Akeem's teacher. And here I was, meeting with his Mom and Uncle, able to tell them of the great progress Akeem had made in a few short months. He was beginning to read, and I was able to give him a placement score for the first time in over a year. He was attempting to write and though below level, he was spelling phonetically, using his letter sounds in ways that made sense. His mom and uncle beamed with pride.

By the end of the year, Akeem was two reading levels behind where the school district wanted him to be moving on to second grade. He was writing in full sentences and able to read and comprehend. He was talking, communicating with his peers and myself, laughing, learning, and growing. I marveled at how cultivating a color brave classroom helped to melt his tough exterior and help instill joy into his life, giving him a voice and place in our classroom.

The last day of school came for this group of Sparkling Scholars. I heard whispering and giggling, mixed with a firm voice just outside my classroom door.

"Go! Go, give to your teacher," I heard the voice say in broken English. I recognized it instantly.

In through the door, being gently pushed in my direction was Akeem carrying a box and note. His mom, carrying his baby sister, and older sister were right behind him coming through the door.

"Here," Akeem said, shoving the beautiful, flowered box and goldenrod yellow envelope into my hand.

I opened the note. Simply written in Akeem's handwriting but with perfect spelling, no doubt helped at home. The note said, *Thank you for everything. Love, Akeem.*

I opened the box. What gift does a Muslim family bring to a young, white teacher to say thank you for all you've done to help their child?

It was a hijab. A beautiful, hand-woven hijab. I lost it, tears falling down my cheeks. I scooped up Akeem and threw my arms around him. My eyes locked with his mom's; her eyes were moist.

Sobbing, she said, "Thank you. Thank you for all you have done for him. We will never forget you." We hugged, tears flowing freely. I knew at that moment I had become color brave.

SPARKLING SCHOLARS

I was raised to believe a false dichotomy. An imaginary and false premise that public school teachers couldn't be a light for Jesus, that they are akin to Hitler's armed forces. Being in this space was guiding me out of this dark cave of belief as the rays of light were breaking through.

One of the components that made me an amazing teacher was, oddly, my homeschool background. I didn't have a previous bias or schema to compare things to, so in a way, I became the theoretical spokesperson for public education. I lived and breathed the theories. I could see clearly how they were intended to be fleshed out in the classroom because I wasn't approaching things with a clouded vision of how things were intended to be based on my experiences in first, fourth, or sixth grade. I only knew how it was supposed to be.

The longer I was a teacher, the more and more convinced I became in my calling. I knew without a doubt that this is what God had called me to do, to be able to reach a child who was facing insurmountable odds at home and needed an advocate. My inner child healed as I stepped in to be for other children what I had needed.

This tender space I had created in my classroom was one of warmth, harmony, and deep levels of learning. We laughed together and loved fiercely. We were a tribe. Over the course of a year, we would cry, love, laugh, and learn together growing into better versions of ourselves than we were when we walked in the doors. Teachers and administrators hated leaving my room. Every observation and walk-through feedback were always the same: *We wish we could watch you teach all day.* I always hated the dreaded observations though and the subsequent feeling of being completely exposed, having yourself on display for critique. The criteria always felt like it was shifting, ambiguous, not objective, and largely based on how the administrator felt when in my room. I hated that part, despite always getting excellent feedback. I wanted concrete outcomes, that if met, meant that I had met the objective and could rest knowing I had done well. The emphasis on constant growth and reflection made it a challenge though because under that premise, no one ever achieves the desired level.

We were on the verge of losing our accreditation status, this district along the Delmar Divide. Our state school board representative was in our building weekly rolling out additional requirements and responsibilities for our school. The leadership team met weekly, a committee where I was a part. We would flesh out how to communicate to staff the increased expectations from our state as well as our new superintendent. It meant increased rigor, scheduling to the minute, objectives written for every lesson, and research-based learning strategies, ensuring that every decision was backed with research and could be supported through a state standard. It looked like lesson plans posted outside your door, test prep classes for our students who's worth would be measured in a score at the end of the year, scripted guiding reading groups and structured centers. More work, more grind, added stress. I never ate lunch and went to the bathroom maybe once a day. There simply wasn't time. Many nights I wouldn't get home until well after eight o'clock trying to accomplish all that was being asked of me, terrified of being a non-tenured teacher who could be let go for any reason, at any time.

And yet, I remained brave. I showed up and taught and loved my first graders. I did what was needed but I challenged the system when my door was closed. My first graders didn't need more grind, they needed to catch the joy of reading. They needed to talk and socialize, they needed to know how to think about   the   deeper meaning of a book and write about their life. They needed a space to play and giggle, grow, and gain.

Statistics have shown that children that live in urban communities and neighborhoods and have high poverty rates often lack access to books that are read to them regularly. This is due in part to the work   schedules of parents and economic resources, and as a result, their acquisition of vocabulary stagnates behind their peers. I looked for ways to help overcome this gap. Word walls in elementary schools were one educational concept that theorists have said helps with this potential gap. Word walls I had observed that were set up by teachers contained sight words that were introduced to young readers. In my experience, they were rarely used by students, and became wallpaper that felt like another chore for a teacher to maintain. I knew things had to be done differently than what I was seeing modeled. I took the risks I needed to innovate, even if that meant I was afraid of what my administration would say.

I was determined. I had my first graders come up with new words every day that they could find that started with a letter of the week. The words they came up with were added to our word wall and I watched their vocabulary grow and expand to new heights. I added sight words and occasionally added some of my own. When we got to the week where we focused on the letter J, one of my sweet little first graders wrote "Jesus." Jesus was on my word wall and a daily reminder of His presence in my classroom for the remainder of that year. I lived in fear that a superintendent or principal would come in and have me take it down or I would get written up, but I remained brave, sure of my calling and purpose.

When my first graders had their opportunity to choose dramatic play for a center choice, something I guarded vigorously in spite of being required to give up seemingly non-academic play, my sweet first graders sat down around their table and prayed over their pretend plates of food. Those same first graders played church and Sunday School. Daily I was humbled to be a part of something that felt bigger than me. Jesus was there in it all, reminding me daily He was in this work and calling. Equipping me, even when it became impossibly hard.

I wasn't prepared for this.

I sat, wide eyed, staring at an angry mom who had brought one of my little boys from the nurse where I had sent him a few minutes earlier. I was in my rocking chair, while reading a book to my first graders who were gathered around me.

"You can just *check his pants!*" she said, inflamed, holding his suspenders.

Stay calm, I reassured myself. My teacher's assistant and I had sent her son to the nurse to get a change of clothes. Bright eyed Xavion needed someone to bring him an extra change of clothes because he was struggling with toileting. This was an issue we had tried to communicate with his parents, but there was a failure to understand the importance of helping him gain independence with this skill. His parents were first generation immigrants but had been here for quite some years, having opened a successful hair salon, specializing in braiding. His mom was called from her shop and had fled out the security door from the office, grabbing Xavion's backpack that had already been sent down, and barged through our closed classroom door. She was infuriated. Coming to school meant doing without money. The language barrier didn't make it easy.

My teacher's assistant, Mrs. Martin and I had come a long way since the beginning of the school year. I was the progressive, hippy flower child of teaching, deceptively lenient to those who didn't know or understand my approach with discipline. She was old-school, no nonsense, and had high expectations. We found commonality in our love of our students, high expectations, and love for Jesus. She became a spiritual mother to me that year, deepening my love for Jesus and trust and reliance on Him.

"No, no we can't check his pants, that isn't something we can do," I stated as reassuringly calm as I could muster. Mrs. Martin heard the falter in my voice.

"Yes, yes you can!" Xavion's mom said, shouting now and approaching the carpet where we were attempting to learn...something. "You should have checked his pants! Look! Nothing!" Hastily, she opened his pants and pointed. Angry darts flew from her eyes.

The situation had escalated. I began to look for exit strategies. Mrs. Martin and I locked eyes and in an instant we knew. She got up and attempted to de-escalate his mom. My phone was clear across the room and my cell phone was on my table. There was no administrator in sight, no one who realized that this parent had slipped out the security door and was now angrily confronting teachers in their classroom in front of sixteen other first graders. My teammates were in their classrooms, unaware that there was a parent creating a threat in the room next to me.

Mrs. Martin approached his mom tentatively and began to engage her in conversation. Expertly, she invited her into the pod just outside our classroom door, offering a listening ear. She again explained that this was not something we could do. She explained that teachers can't check student's pants and reiterated that when the nurse determines they need to be sent home, that there is nothing we can do to argue that point. Still fuming, she was noticeably calmer, and Mrs. Martin was able to walk her out the door to the parking lot.

My heart racing, I wondered. Why didn't the office know she left the secured area? We had video cameras in the hallways with front desk monitors. Where was administration and where was the secretary? Where was the support? I had an intruder in my room, confronting me, yelling at me and my assistant for a decision that wasn't ours. This could have gone so much worse! What if it had been a different parent that was armed? My heartbeat faster, my anxiety kicking in.

Deep breaths. I had sixteen little six-year-olds to reassure and my racing mind wandered back to them. I had to get us back on track. This machine stopped for nothing.

LEFT BEHIND

You could feel the anxiety and tension rising in the building as the pressure of state accreditation loomed on the horizon. Daily, my coworkers and I would glance at each other when passing in the hallway and shake our heads. Deep sighs. Heaviness. Invisible burdens on our shoulders that felt impossible to bear. Impossible gaps to overcome. State mandates and the looming dread of the standardized end of year assessment were beckoning us all like a judgment day. We knew that if collectively, we didn't raise the bar, we would be exchanging a paycheck for a pink slip. Out of 26 teachers on staff, nearly 40% of us were non-tenured.

Parents would show up, unannounced when phone calls were made regarding student behavior. Disliking the content of the conversation they had had with their child's teacher; they would show up and yell at our secretary, who was one of the strongest women I knew, demanding to speak with our principal. Our secretary was unflinching in the face of the verbal onslaught. The principal gave these parents the opportunity to be heard and chastised my coworkers regularly, adding to the burgeoning dread that you could feel up and down the parking lot as we piled out of our cars, walking into the building. By December of my last year, everyone was looking to leave. No one was unscathed.

January loomed over the dawn of the coming Christmas break and with it, our school district's mid-year data points that would be used by the State of Missouri to assess our district's accreditation status at the end of the year. Daily teaching life consisted of writing scripted lesson plans, walk-throughs with extensive reflection forms, and submitting data on student goals. High stakes testing was required weekly. As teachers we were expected to raise our students' reading levels. These levels were predetermined benchmarks set by the district and our state. Every strategy we used had to be backed by research. We had to submit anecdotal notes, meet with instructional coaches, attend professional development, and strive to help students be at or above these predetermined reading levels to help with learning gaps. Learning gaps that were there before we arrived. We were expected to address the myriad of complex issues that can interfere with a student's ability to learn. The unspoken expectation was that we would be miracle workers within a system that felt inhumane, developmentally inappropriate, and unnatural.

Kehlani came into my room, in tears and wearing what she had on yesterday.

"Ms. Hawkins, I didn't sleep last night," she trembled as she collapsed into my arms needing to be held. Dirt covered her tear-streaked face. Her normally buoyant hair was matted. Blood streaked her knees.

I prompted my class to begin working on their words or to read a book from their book boxes. I sensed it was going to be a long morning.

"What happened?" I asked, as I rocked her.

She melted, her little shoulders heaving, bearing some unspoken burden.

I pressed a bit harder. "Do you want to tell me about it?"

Breathless, she gestured "no," with her head. Minutes passed. I rocked and prayed she would open up. She had a hard life and a huge heart, for a six-year-old. I frequently caught her taking things from the classroom to give to her younger brothers and sisters. Too shaken to speak, I asked if she wanted to see our counselor. She shook her head "no," once more. I asked her if she wanted to write it down, an activity she loved to do. She would often pour her heart out writing pages and pages, taking hours to illustrate the worlds she penned. Finally, I got a nod of "yes."

Relieved, I set her up at the writing table letting her process while I corralled the two boys who were on the verge of a full-blown UFC wrestling match in the back of the classroom. Their puppets were wrestling, they reassured me, their twinkling brown eyes betraying them. *I didn't know a shark and squirrel could fight,* I thought to myself.

After attendance and morning announcements, she found me. By then Mrs. Martin was there to take over. Kehlani handed me her story. There was no writing, just a picture of a police car, red and blue sirens, a young boy lying down, two little girls, and a gun. I stared into her wide brown eyes, big and frightened like a doe's.

"My brother was...arrested...last...night...," she spilled, crying once again. Mrs. Martin and I locked eyes from across the room as I hugged her. "They threw him to the ground and took him to jail," she continued, weeping. "And my Granny is coming because they are gonna take us away." She buried her face on my shoulder. I picked her up and rubbed her back.

"How old is your brother?" I asked.

"Seventeen," she said. "I tried to stop them from taking him away. That's when I fell." She rubbed her knee. Just a couple hours later, the office called. I was shaken. So many layers of trauma wrapped up in this recounted tale. A tale too often repeated and thought of as routine. I felt helpless. She needed a school day to pause, and someone in her life to be a safe place to process with. She needed a counselor to be available to help her unpack her trauma. She needed resources we didn't have. What she got was the best we could offer, but it wasn't enough. We didn't help her unpack her trauma and instead, she packed her backpack.

"Ms. Hawkins? Yes, it's Ms. Sunday. Kehlani's Granny is here to get her. She'll need to bring her things." She hung up.

I gathered Kehlani and gave her a puppet. I just knew in my heart this would be the last time I saw her. I wrapped her in a big hug. I told her how much I loved her and walked her to the office. I had to go to the bathroom to wipe the tears from my eyes.

She didn't return. Granny had come to take her and her little sister back to Texas. The next day, me and my coworkers began to process the grief of losing these two little girls. We held each other, hugged each other, and cried together. Senseless injustice, a traumatized family, and teachers who dealt with the aftermath, feeling powerless. We knew what these little girls had said, we knew what they needed, and yet- they were forgotten by a system. Pouring your heart and soul into children and having no way to say goodbye was crushing.

Pouring your heart and soul into children who were traumatized and lacked resources to help their lives was demoralizing.

As the year progressed, I had a parent who was determined to stick around in my classroom well past drop-off hours. She would stay, bring her son McDonald's breakfast to eat in the classroom, and do all of his morning work for him. Writing was hard for him, and he did not want to work independently. Daily, she would arrive late. She would linger until 10:30 or sometimes 11:00. No background check was required of her, no visitor pass to indicate who she was. Our building policy was clear: no parents were to linger past 8:30 am without a background check and visitors pass. Despite my principal escorting her out early on in the school year and my admonitions to leave, she continued to stay. Throughout the year, this continued. Her son grew to the point where he wouldn't work or participate, and his mom began speaking to and instructing my other students. Despite asking for support from administration, my requests went unnoticed. The response was, "We have an open-door policy for parents." End of discussion.

It was incredibly stressful to teach with such parental scrutiny, on top of the near daily administrative walk-throughs and critiques. Teaching truly is a work of heart, as the saying goes. After driving a ninety-minute commute every morning for the last year and a half, stressed about making it to school on time, I began to experience significant impacts to my health. Contracts were going to be given out in January, and we all felt the collective pressure to perform, perform, perform. Paranoia ran high among my colleagues, who would often be in my room to vent. They always asked me to unplug my phone in case we were being listened to. I never felt that our principal would even have time to do that, but they could not be convinced.

One morning in December, I pulled into the parking lot and my symptoms felt all too familiar. I felt like I had been hit by a train once again. My head was pounding and despite having taken something for my headache before I left the house, I now only felt worse. My heart was racing. I walked to my classroom, leaving the lights off. I knew something wasn't right, but my Sparkling Scholars were arriving soon. I muddled through the morning, dropping them off at music class. My vision blacked out and I felt nauseous. I went to the nurse and told her my symptoms. She placed the blood pressure cuff on my arm. It tightened. I knew it was bad.

"177/119," She said kindly, looking into my eyes on the table. "If you were 180 over 120, I would need to call an ambulance. You need to call your doctor and see if you can leave." She must have seen the worry in my eyes. "Why don't you rest here a bit and then I'll recheck it." I attempted to rest, but my mind raced. *I need a sub; I can't teach like this!* I thought as my heart raced. *What if I pass out? I need to call my doctor...I have to go pick up my scholars in a few minutes...What am I going to do?*

The second reading of my blood pressure was still the same, so off I went to the secretary to inform her I needed a sub and why I needed to go home.

"I'm sorry, Ms. Hawkins, but we don't have any subs today," she stated, matter of fact. Her assertiveness threw me off.

"What? I need to be able to go home and get to the doctor!" I panicked. *What if I have to stay here all day long?*

"We don't have any building subs today," she reiterated. "You can ask Mrs. Thompson if you can take off but I don't have any subs for you. You'll be ok." Her reassurance was...touching. Touching some parts of my heart that for sure felt hot at the indifference. Crestfallen, tears flowed down my cheeks. I knew this was a serious health risk, yet no one cared. *I need to go and find Mrs. Thompson. I need to call my doctor!*

I spent the rest of my plan time on hold with the doctor's office and I never made it through their line in the limited time I had left. They were on lunch break when I had my plan time. I held on listening through the repetitious, irritating waiting-line music for over half an hour. I hung up the phone. With no doctor's advice or order to leave, I was in a   desperate situation. The nurse came back to check on me, asking if I could leave. I told her the situation. She looked as helpless as I felt.

I found my coworkers, tearful, and explained my situation. They were incensed that I was being asked to stay and work through this health crisis. I didn't have my Mrs. Martin; she was out for the day and there was no one to replace her. This meant I had no one to cover my class. Soon, I was dropping my first graders off in my second-grade coworkers' room so I could attempt to get a hold of my doctor yet again.

We're sorry, all of our representatives are busy taking another call-click. I didn't have time. I attempted to find my principal only to see her in a meeting.

I muddled through the day, lights off, played movies and worried. I worried about what would happen to my kids if I passed out in a room with a school that was short staffed. I had a conversation with them about calling 911 and going to the office in the case of an emergency. They were blissfully unaware that I was seriously sick, they thought it was a fun movie day. I tried to call my doctor throughout the day and each time it was clear their phone lines were down. The end of the day came, but by the time I got to my car, which was as soon as my contracted time would allow, my doctor's office had closed for the day. I jotted the number down, but I was furious. This system was breaking me. Having a health crisis was not compatible with this broken educational system. I called my NEA representative for my district and told her what I was going through. I wanted it on record. She told me to document this and shared with me that she was sorry. She said she was going to reach out to a lawyer to discuss my rights. I told her I would follow up with her in a few days. I picked up the phone and called the emergency after hours number.

I merged onto Interstate I-55, a major interstate connecting Memphis and St. Louis, in the final leg of my ninety-minute commute. Ironically, this interstate had just been renamed the Ruby Bridges highway, replacing its KKK namesake just a year before Michael Brown was shot. This tragedy never escaped my attention. Daily, I felt the racism enshroud the southern Jefferson county line, like a demonic stronghold.

Attempting to call yet again, I finally got through to an after-hours nurse. She began to ask me questions, attempting to diagnose my symptoms. As she was talking to me, I felt the hand that was holding my phone go numb. I dropped the phone. I blacked out.

"Hello? Ms. Hawkins?" I heard a voice say, as I recovered and placed the phone back to my ear.

"Yes, I'm here. I blacked out," I said weakly. I veered off to the shoulder and put the phone on speaker as I turned my emergency flashers on.

"Ma'am, you need to get to a place where you are safe. You need to call an ambulance to get you to the nearest emergency room." I could hear the urgency in her voice.

"Ok, I am pulling off now."

"I'm going to stay on the phone with you until you make it to safety, ok?"

Praying through panic, I made it to safety and then later arrived at the emergency room. I got the full work-up. I was diagnosed with stress-related hypertension and was placed on anti-anxiety and blood pressure medication. I knew when I left that hospital that I was going to have to leave my school. I knew that I would not be able to survive here. This place was quite literally, as the Fugees put it, "killing me softly."

The situation with Ronnie's mom came to a head in the spring. His behavior and insistence that he didn't need to listen to any teacher "I don't like," as he would say, led to the assault of one of my coworkers, a sweet paraprofessional whose very presence lit up our entire school with joy and positivity. We were scheduled to attend a field trip the day after this incident occurred. When I picked him up from music and discovered what he had done, I told my principal my concerns about his escalating behavior. I explained how he had assaulted my paraprofessional and then ran out of the room because he felt he did not have to listen. She told me that Ronnie would not be able to go on the field trip unless he was accompanied by his mom. This seemed reasonable. If that was not a possibility, then he would be unable to go due to safety concerns. She told me to inform his mom. I thought this was odd, considering discipline decisions rest with administration and it is administration who informs parents when a disciplinary decision has been made. These decisions do not rest with teachers. This wasn't the first time that this had happened, where something the principal should have done fell on my shoulders. Being a young teacher, I should have read the room better in this situation. I typed the email, copied my principal on it, and informed his mom of what he had done and the consequences of it.

I showed up to work the next morning, an hour early. His mom was there, in the parking lot. She was walking the doors of the school, clearly agitated. There was hardly anyone in the parking lot, so I left and chose to go get coffee. Her body language made me uncomfortable. I had informed his mom over email but had not received a response from her. *Maybe if I leave and come back she will be gone.* Hard pass. She was clearly upset. I pulled back into the school parking lot to see her walk up to my principal's car. She began to engage with Mrs. Thompson, yelling at her as she was walking into the building. Once they were inside, I went to my kindergarten teachers' classrooms on the other side of the building to stay hidden until school started. I knew she would be in my room but there was no way that I was going to subject myself to being harassed or verbally assaulted. I told my coworkers what was going on. They said they overheard her threatening me, wanting to "fight." My principal deescalated the situation, by giving his mom what she wanted: for her son to attend a field trip without her (when she had been present every morning prior) and to not miss out due to the fact that he assaulted a staff member who was nearly his size and weight. My words held no more meaning; my legs had been cut off from underneath me.

This was truly the last straw for me. As torn and conflicted as I was about leaving my sweet community of kids in the Delmar Divide, and as conflicted as I was knowing just how much they needed excellent teachers, I knew I could no longer fill that role. The stress was killing me quite literally and with it, stealing my joy. I knew I needed to use my gifts elsewhere, even if I felt I was leaving these kids- my kids- behind.

INVISIBLE CHILDREN

*"Education is not a way to escape poverty,
it is a way of fighting it."*
-Julius Nyerere

I had been playing down by the pond and was desperate for a drink of water. The humidity was thick enough to cut with a knife. Sweat beaded around my crimson face. I hated that I got red-faced in the summer. Everyone always asked me, "Why is your face so red? Are you ok?" I wanted to slink away and hide, generally mortified at how much I resembled Bob the Tomato, a character from *Veggie Tales*. If I knew then what I know now, I would have quipped, "Because I'm white!" As it was, I did my best to be discreet. As discreet as my loudmouth and red face would allow.

I ran up our acre-long steep hill, sun beating down on my face while little streams of sweat rolled down it. I pushed through the heat until I got to the shaded carport and saw a minivan in our driveway. I knew whose minivan it was. Anne, a young homeschool mom, had been having issues with her husband for weeks. I knew because my mom had been spending four to six hours a day on the phone with her, giving her counsel and listening to her situation. It was impossible not to hear what was going on, being in the house, trying to teach myself from my fifth grade ABeka math book at eleven, darting underneath and around the stretched out, coiled phone cord line for much of the day. Some days I fantasized about clicking on the hang-up button. One time I actually did. The price that my backside paid was almost worth it.

My mom was seen as a spiritual advisor in our homeschool community. People sought her out to talk to and to get spiritual advice and insight. Most notably, women that were in abusive marriages. My mom had stayed with my dad, citing that her faithfulness in staying married to him was a testimony of God's grace, healing, and restoration. It didn't matter that he had dark, hidden addictions, she believed praying and being submissive to him saved her marriage. She encouraged others with her testimony, and many times, encouraged women to try to be submissive to their husbands and stay married, even under abusive circumstances. Her favorite verse to use for women she spoke to was I Peter 3:1. It was outlined, highlighted, and annotated in her Bible.

Wives in the same way submit yourselves to your own husbands so that, if any of them do not believe the word, they may be won over without words by the behavior of their wives (NIV).

I pushed through the side door from the carport and felt the cold air hit me as I opened it. Something in the room was off. Anne's two little boys, around five and six, were playing with my little brother's GI Joes on the living room floor. She sat at our kitchen table, visibly shaken and noticeably pregnant. Her thick black hair disheveled, she had big purple bruises on her eye and cheekbone, dark marks on her arms, tears running down her cheeks and falling on her belly. The atmosphere was broken, the air felt depressing. I grabbed my water and ran back to my room and shut the door. I needed a haven from this.

Even at eleven, I knew this wasn't right. I didn't have the words to describe what I saw, but it felt like a crime scene. I sat, still as a mouse on the other side of my closed bedroom door and listened to the hushed conversation hoping to hear a voice of truth, confirming what my young heart already knew. A voice of reason, telling her to get away and to be safe.

"I...had...get...away...from...didn't...where...to go..." I strained my ears. I could barely make out the words at the end of the hallway, even with my ear pressed against the door.

"God...honors...submission...He...help you..." my mom responded.

I was infuriated. How could my mom encourage her to stay? To submit when it was obvious she was hurt? She had bruises on her face and arms! Anne and her boys stayed for the rest of the day and left right before my dad came home. About a week later, she called my mom again. This time, the tears ran down my mom's cheeks.

Her unborn baby died at six months gestation.

No police report was ever filed, no social worker was allowed to investigate because DFS was refused entry to their home. Anne had joined HSLDA, known as the Homeschool Legal Defense Organization, an organization with the express interest of preserving parental rights to homeschool in America. She had called the lawyers on staff who told the workers to go away. Anne would go on to have another baby, fully convinced that her marriage had been restored by her submission. Tragically, this wasn't the only act of domestic violence I was impacted by. Another family that we were very close to and spent a lot of time with growing up, often doing homeschool classes together, had an alcoholic father. He would rage and throw objects at his wife and two children. She too, showed up eight months pregnant at our house, having bruises on her arms, telling my mom that she too, had been beaten. Miraculously, her baby lived. They too, had more children after this, all in the name of a marriage healed by the Holy Spirit- and submission. This incident happened just months before Anne's baby died, no doubt my mom considered it a testament to God's healing power.

Just two short years later, when I was thirteen, my own world came crashing down around me and not a soul knew outside my immediate family. I finally had the courage to tell my Grandma almost fifteen years later. I carried a secret about myself into adulthood although it was far from forgotten in my mind. A secret, I was told not to talk about.

When I was thirteen, I attempted suicide. It was a result of over a year of Cynthia informing the other families within the Movement to keep their daughters away from me due to the fact that I had become an ungodly influence. I was growing in my personality at thirteen and was finding my voice, asserting my opinions. I was publicly shunned. My former friends would see me approach them and walk away. Sometimes, even wiping the dust from the heels of their shoes as they turned their backs. Eliza would openly invite others to social functions and parties and would intentionally say in front of the group to me, "You're not invited." No explanation was given. In the days before cyber bullying, this was about as classic of an example of bullying and mean girls as you got. I was an extraverted, social butterfly who loved her friends and a good laugh. I didn't understand why suddenly no one wanted to be my friend. I internalized it, wondering if it was something I had done. After months of crying about this to my mom, crushed to be so shunned and disincluded, my mom met with Cynthia to see what the issue was with Eliza and me.

After my mom met with Cynthia, her demeanor towards me had changed. She came home angry, refusing to speak to me for a week. I would ask her about what she and Cynthia talked about, and she would tell me she needed to pray about what to say to me. One week later, she and my dad moved the living room furniture around and informed me they were going to speak with me later that night. It felt...wrong. Our furniture *never* got rearranged. We always ate in the same seats at the dining room table. The fact that the two La-Z-Boy recliners were pulled facing the sofa into a circle, felt like an inquisition was about to take place. When my brother was in bed, my mom pulled out an 8 ½ x 11-inch, yellow legal pad. On every page was Cynthia's handwriting. My mom began to accuse me of sins against the Movement and against Eliza, reading from this notepad the incidents that Cynthia had captured about me for the last year and a half.

"Chandra is too loud when there are groups and adults speaking."

"Her laugh is too loud, not the mark of a quiet and gentle spirit."

"She gossips."

"Chandra contradicts adults."

"Chandra is disrespectful."

"She told Eliza her hair was longer than hers."

And on it went, specifics, dates and times were included. Incident after incident was read to me. At the end, my mom concluded with scripture, highlighting how I was not a godly young woman and a disgrace to the Movement. She said that because I was disrespectful and didn't have a quiet and gentle spirit, that my former friends' parents were instructed to keep their girls from me, so that I would not corrupt them. And my parents, wanting to keep their status in the Movement, sided with Cynthia and determined to correct me. I was informed that I would have to show marks of improvement, or I would continue to have no friends, fully and completely isolated from any of the outside world.

My world was gone, crashing down around my feet. I felt completely beaten and not a hand was raised. I was berated and my soul felt dead, my life felt bleak and worthless. The amount of shame I bore was crushing. Red faced, crying, and panicking I realized I would never be able to meet the mark of the idealism that my parents and the Movement was exacting upon me. I couldn't change my personality and I couldn't change my laugh. Yet in order to have friends, something that every thirteen-year-old girl desires, that is precisely what I was going to be asked to do. My spirit was crushed.

So, I slammed doors, cried, and ran off. I ran to the only room in the house that had a lock on it- my parents' bedroom. I locked the door behind me as I slammed it shut, the sound reverberating off the walls of the house, even shaking the windows.

Dad's gun. I wanted my life to be over. I was being verbally assaulted and emotionally abused in my own home, and no one knew. My parents were knocking on the other side of the door, but my nearly seven-foot father wasn't too intent on forcing it open.

I opened the filing cabinet and pulled out the .357, placing my hand on the trigger. It was loaded. I unlocked it and held the gun, staring at the barrel in front of me, while tears were streaming down my face. I wanted my life to be over, I wanted all this pain to end. *One...two...three...*

An invisible hand placed my gun-bearing one on the bed. I looked up. Nothing. No one was there.

I picked the gun up again, against the backdrop of clamoring on the other side. If time stood still, it quite possibly did. Once again, my hand was moved to the bed by an invisible God with measurable force.

For I know the plans I have for you, Chandra. Plans to give you hope and a future. I froze. I didn't know how there were these miraculous forces at work in this moment, and my reality hadn't changed, but in that moment I knew I wasn't alone. I was seen.

The rest of my homeschool high school experience consisted of spiritually abusive lectures, where my mom would use the Bible to tell me how far from the mark of favor I had fallen. These happened daily. I was chronically depressed and cried myself to sleep every night. I was told in no uncertain terms by my parents that I was not to share this incident with anyone, especially my grandparents. The abuse I experienced as a child was hidden.

We never spoke about the baby who died tragically because his mom was beaten so harshly. We never spoke about the kids that were trapped in unsafe homes, invisible from a world who could help them, hidden and forgotten. We never spoke again of my suicide attempt and what help I was crying out for. We never spoke of the fact that I had pneumonia, nearly died, and would have vanished from existence, barely noticed. Gaslighting was a powerful force at work. Keeping children invisible was the logical conclusion of corrupt, absolute, parental power that lacked accountability.

I watched the green pastures roll by and noticed fog was covering the rolling Missouri mountains as I drove to work. I had successfully landed a position that still required a commute, but it was now only 45 minutes instead of the hour and a half I had spent daily in the car for the last two years. It felt cathartic to have this place to work, where the pace felt slower, less urgent. It felt like getting in touch with my country roots, and once again, my heart healed as I reconnected with cows, hay bales, and green rolling hills in Southern Missouri on my daily drive.

Teaching in a rural school district wasn't what I expected, although if you asked me at the time, I wouldn't have been able to articulate what my expectations were. I remember talking to one of my district supervisors about teaching in the Delmar Divide and the experiences I had there, early on in the hiring process. "Oh, I think we will surprise you how much we are alike," she said with a gentle laugh. I couldn't process how on earth two districts that were 50 miles apart, serving two student demographics that were on apparent opposite sides of life's equation could be similar. It didn't take long to find out.

While I was student teaching, I chose to diversify my experience and student taught in a thimble-sized rural school, where mud caked the floors, and no air conditioning was installed in buildings. Every spring, windows had to be opened. The smell of the sewer plant just behind the parking lot filled the classroom air. Students wore cowboy boots more than sneakers, deer season was a school holiday, and finding construction paper on hand was like striking gold. My mentor was a veteran and had learned to save everything. She had spent her life here, in a township of 5,000. She shared her heart with me frequently, about how forgotten she felt her students were and how resources should be spread equitably among all schools, regardless of zip code to give every child a fair chance, regardless of socio-economic status. The teachers in this school made nearly ten thousand less than a larger, neighboring district, and resources meant a lot to this little school district. I was just beginning to learn about how systemic poverty was. That was nearly four years ago from the moment I found myself in now, preparing to teach my new group of third graders.

I was in love with teaching third graders, even though the pressure of standardized testing was a new added element. I loved it most because we shared the beauty of chapter books together. My lessons were centered around a book, and I read each book with theatrics, inflection, and high-level questions to help my Sparkling Scholars develop their listening comprehension. We laughed together, cried together, and met each other on the carpet in my classroom. When I was reading, lines blurred, defenses of the most challenging students were down, we were vulnerable, and we thought deeply. Katherine Applegate, Kate DiCamillo, Lois Lowry, Jacqueline Woodson, Sharon Creech, Peter Brown, and others taught us life-giving lessons and we were once again knit together.

One powerful novel we read as a class was Katherine Applegate's, *Crenshaw*. It is an amazing work of literary art, drawing attention to homelessness and the coping strategies that children who live in poverty sometimes use. In it, the protagonist, Jackson, finds an imaginary cat, Crenshaw, who helps him during some bleak days that his family must face while being homeless. It's a story of resilience and realistic hope under hardships.

What I didn't realize when I chose this book for my students was the backstory of students in my classroom who were facing the harsh realities of rural poverty. As I began reading this book, I knew on a surface level what my students were facing but I didn't understand it in depth. In talking with my friend and school counselor, and as students opened up and shared with me, I realized that this was how these two parts of America were actually the same. Students in both districts I had taught faced insurmountable odds, and the impact poverty had on them was similar. It truly was two different sides of the same coin.

Drugs impacted both family dynamics, and while marijuana was prevalent in the city, opioids were the drug of choice here, arguably the more detrimental of the two. Both drugs though held the potential to destroy families and robbed them of life-giving opportunities. Often, their children were left fending for themselves in these scenarios. Both worlds wanted their kids to have the opportunity to have an education, realizing its importance in rising above the circumstances that life had thrown at them.

Joblessness impacted both sectors, which compounded housing issues. Finding a job, and finding reliable transportation that was affordable, were enormous factors. Transportation was easier to come by in the city, so parents in the city had more options. What bus system was going to take my student's parents to St. Louis or a larger neighboring county to find a job when they lived an hour away from a major metropolitan area? In the city, my students who were homeless qualified for taxi services to get to school so at least they had a way there, provided they woke up on time and were helped out the door. Here, my homeless students either had to find a bus to ride, walk to school, or skip school entirely. Sometimes our school counselor or principal would pick them up and bring them to school but with so many, that wasn't always possible.

Housing impacted both worlds, but my students who were homeless in the city were always cleaner. I started asking why, and when I was receptive enough for the answer, I found it. Housing shelters, running water, and heat were far more accessible in the city. We had no housing shelters in Farmington. Instead of a night in a shelter, my homeless students spent nights on the streets of a small town, with sheets of metal, plywood, and pallets for makeshift lean-tos. Small space heaters would be plugged into a source to attempt heating. No running water, no heating, no shelter. I was thankful to have a classroom they felt safe enough to fall asleep in.

The longer I taught here the more I realized how impactful poverty was on a child's life. I felt like I was running an orphanage much of the time, while teaching in both districts. I was always making sure my kids had food, they were warm and had coats, hats, and gloves, that they knew they were loved and cared for. Finding books for them to read, providing laughter to lighten the burden on their young shoulders were other duties I joyfully performed in my "orphanages." Kids in poverty have issues that they generally did not attempt to hide and yet were treated as though they were invisible. Their issues remain unseen and unanswered by willful ignorance. Sure, think tanks and theorists have hypothesized the impacts of urban and rural poverty. But what is ever done about it? Besides making sure that every child has free breakfast and lunch? What were we doing to help lift this child and their parents out of homelessness? Out of joblessness? How were we ensuring free, public transportation? The answers are bigger than our bravery.

What Katherine Applegate did in her book, *Crenshaw,* was highlight the fact that there is a fine line that families walk between homelessness and lower-class status. It happened quickly to Jackson's family, and it wasn't because of a mental illness that his family ended up that way. It wasn't because they were bad with money or any other societal stigma we attach to homelessness and poverty-stricken families. No, it was simply, they didn't have enough resources to cover emergency expenses and life sometimes throws you lemons.

Crenshaw taught me and my students to look deeper and that there are invisible stories you can't see until the eyes of your heart are open to see them. There are children who are invisible, fighting domestic violence behind a structure that facilitates and harbors it, forgotten children to society. There are children who are invisible to us, fighting to get to school after having slept in a shelter, abandoned building, or in a cardboard box. Their bravery to speak out against abuse or their bravery to wade through layers of structural dysfunction just to get to school every morning should be met with the same bravery in us. Bravery to have the hard conversations, to report the abuse when we reasonably suspect it, and to do more than point to a job board or run a food pantry drive as a solution to their struggles. Giving these children an education is, as the quote I used earlier in the chapter says, only one weapon we can equip them with to fight poverty. They need more than that if they are going to escape it. Maybe we shouldn't be so quick to think about building starships that get us to Mars and think about ways we can build avenues and infrastructure that supports the invisible children that fight battles we don't see, every single day.

THE LAST BATTLE

Growing up homeschooled, I had a very simplistic view of money that was handed to me. My understanding of finances and the cost of a dollar was skewed to say the least. It was odd because my father was in finance. My parents clearly never had money, but they raised me with the false idea that if you tithed to a local church (a concept of giving ten percent and in turn God would bless you), saved a certain percent of your income, didn't take government handouts, and watched your spending you would have all you needed to be financially stable in life. I grew up watching my mom never engage with finances because it was my dad's profession, and he was the head of the household. I came into marriage with that same premise, and it was through my years working as a professionally educated woman that I realized (over the course of time) how naive that thinking was.

My dad was the walking image of Wall Street success. He polished his black, cognac, and merlot colored, size 16 Cole Haan loafers every Sunday. The Wall Street Journal and Barron's were subscriptions that filled the table and magazine racks. His mahogany briefcase that he carried daily felt symbolic of success. He wore custom suits and drove a hunter green Lincoln Continental. Years later, when I was watching *The Family Man* with Nicolas Cage, the scene where the character Jack wanted to spend all of his family's money on a custom suit sickened me. It wasn't funny because that was my real life. Every Christmas, my mom would forgo her Christmas money to ensure that my dad had one or two custom suits, and at nearly seven feet tall they weren't cheap. This is what financial success was supposed to look like. That image handicapped me as I grew into adulthood.

For the first time in my life as a professional woman, I was valued for my intelligence and my contribution. Earning my degree and going to work was one of the most empowering things I had done to date. As I developed my professional identity and recognized my value within a school, I realized that the people in my life who had censored me and tried to keep me from taking up space were wrong. I realized, as I sat in countless professional development conferences where we discussed childhood ACE scores (known as Adverse Childhood Experiences), and how trauma, abuse, and domestic violence impacts children, that my ACE score was impacting me and my boys too.

I realized that I had something of value and worth to contribute to the lives of those around me. I realized that the years of listening to my husband berating me, telling me I was "stupid" and "ignorant" were lies. I wasn't stupid, I was seen and valued by my supervisors and fellow teachers for my intelligence. I also realized the power of my worth.

The cloud began to slowly lift. I realized that it was abusive to set a limit on someone's debit card, to cancel credit cards without consultation, and not allow me to have anything in my name. I realized how insane it was to stalk someone to the store they were going to, show up in a parking lot, and yell at you for purchasing even one item not on his approved list. I began to realize too, that our income had doubled, my lifestyle and spending habits remained the same, and we never had money to spare. I would live in dread, going to the grocery store or getting clothes for my boys. I would wait and pray he wouldn't see the bank account because whenever he did he would leave early from work, screech his wheels into the driveway, and come into the house screaming at me. I lived in fear of being beaten, although he never did. Most days, I wished he would have beaten me because that would have been easier to handle than the mental torment I was living in. His need to control my spending, the money I was making, and my daily decisions were alarming me. This wasn't how other coworkers' relationships were. I now had comparisons of what healthy families looked like, and I knew that this wasn't it. My reality was all too familiar to what I had witnessed growing up, and I knew now it was not how life was supposed to be lived. It wasn't how I wanted to live the rest of my life.

As I learned more about abuse and trauma and domestic violence, I realized I couldn't stay in this relationship. I knew I had to free myself once again and this time, I was freeing my boys too from a toxic home where shouting, screaming, and a battered mom were daily occurrences. I began with therapy for myself. I knew I needed to move quickly, and I wasn't playing around. I didn't care how much money I had to spend; I knew I needed to invest in myself. So, I did.

Katherine and I met weekly, sometimes twice a week. Besides putting myself through school and subbing full-time while being a young momma, I had never worked so hard to get myself healthy and truly free from the mental hold that toxic and abusive people still had on me. I realized my co-dependency, she helped me to see and uncover his narcissism and my empathy. She helped me recover from years of sexual, emotional, mental, and verbal abuse.

Together, we walked the tracks of my mind and plowed ground that would allow me to break free.

And that's when it began to hit me. The years I had spent naively disengaged from our finances, never putting two and two together changed. The man I had been married to had been using drugs our entire marriage and we never had money because he was spending the money I was making on drugs, pulling out cash and getting high on company time. He had never quit using. I was dealing with a spouse who wasn't afraid to lie and manipulate, and someone who was aggressive and abusive. Leaving him required years of planning, preparation, and a swift exit. I separated from him in all aspects except our living arrangements and he never even knew. For two years, I remodeled my home and prepared to sell it, wanting to move back to St. Louis where my friends, church, and community were. I spent two years purging the 16 years of building a life with kids. Alone, I hired a lawyer. I stored everything of value that I wanted, packed away safely in a storage unit. I got my own bank account and realized I had money to make it work.

I picked up the phone and called the number, nervously excited. It was a big step for me. For years, I heard how our home would never sell and we could never get the price for it that we needed. It had been his way of coercive control over my life, keeping me effectively isolated from friends and family.

It also kept me from realizing a dream of a better home in a better area with a better school district. Today was different. I called the number and spoke to an agent who was willing to come and meet with me about my home. I didn't wait for his permission, I listed it. The day the sign was placed in the yard when I pulled in the driveway after a full day of teaching, I wept. That sign represented so much of my personal evolution, having morphed into a powerful, independent woman. That sign represented my freedom.

I was stunned. My home sold in six days and above the asking price. My real estate agent and myself had prepared for it to be on the market through the spring, buying us time to get the boys through the rest of their school year. The timing didn't appear to be the best. Life moves on though, as the saying goes, and the boys and me settled moving back to St. Louis. It meant leaving my Sparkling Scholars and work family in Farmington mid-year, staying would have meant hours in the car commuting. What was astonishing to me was the level of emotional support I received from my administrators, my colleagues, and the school board when I told them what was going on in my personal life. They knew the depth of what I had been going through the last two years and they knew the danger I had been in at times, even offering to write a safety plan for me to ensure my ex wouldn't harass me at work. They knew how to do things well, how to support teachers who were having a personal crisis, and still make sure that learning was happening. The day I left was the hardest day in my professional career to date. Their response, care, concern, love, and support for me and my boys taught me how school leadership can support teachers and their students during a crisis. That was December of 2019.

My boys began to get settled into their new, much larger, but top-performing high school in St. Louis. It wasn't an easy transition by any means, new academic rigor they weren't used to, new teachers, new friend groups. I was committed to helping them adjust and poured myself into them, ensuring that they had all the support they needed to navigate this transition before attempting to look for another position in a couple of months.

From the time I became a teacher, I wanted to teach in St. Louis public schools. Notorious for being a failing district, poor student outcomes, and a sad number of schools that were not accredited, it didn't faze me. I wanted to make an impact and transform the lives of students who deserved a great teacher. That following February, February of 2020, I applied to teach at a sweet little early childhood Magnet school. They believed in the power of a child's voice, choice, and agency. The principal called me and asked me to come and interview later that month. After my interview, I received a phone call to come in and teach a lesson to the kindergarten class I would be taking over for the end of the year.

I walked into the classroom and was greeted instantly with eager smiles and faces. These kindergarteners were eager to have a new teacher, apparently they had had several teachers during the course of this year. They were all seated at their tables, in groups, and in their chairs. That wasn't my teaching style though. I preferred teaching on a carpet where it felt more relational. I carefully set the stage and asked them to come to the carpet. They did great. Until I pulled a book out of my box to introduce to them. There were hardly any books in this barren room, and it was as if they had never seen a book before. I had ten five-year-olds in my lap, all at once.

"Whoa, whoa, whoa!" I chuckled. "I need you on the *edge* of the carpet so everyone can see," I prompted. I started listing the names of the little people who were being leaders and making strong choices. One little boy, Darrian, remained next to me. He had a teacher's assistant with him to support him. He was adorable, and round all over. He had bright sparkly eyes, brown, and shaped like a half-moon. His hair was closely shaved to his head, and he was wearing little red suspenders that held up his blue jeans.

I dove into teaching my lesson on nonfiction text features to these eager, hungry to learn-and-love little people. We talked about the features of the text I was reading from, enjoyed the pictures, and Darrian continued to sit quietly next to me, until he wasn't.

"Ow, ow, oooowwww!" Darrian cried.

I turned. The assistant principal, teachers, and teacher's assistant stayed in the back as I glanced up. It was clear they didn't hear. "What's wrong?" I said, investigating. He was twisted in a strange position and was next to the miniature wooden rocking chair that I thought had been in the corner rather than right next to him.

He grew louder. "OW, OWWW, OWWW! It's stuck. It's *stuuuck*. It's STUCK!"

He was wailing at this point. I told my class of kindergarteners to stay seated amidst their concern and to give him space. I began to see if I could dislodge his very pudgy finger that he had decided was a good idea to stick in between the wooden slats of this small rocking chair. I attempted to slide it out, while the adults looked on, unsure of how to proceed. This was real life, and a real-life interview lesson was taking place. As soon as I attempted to move it, he howled. That was the cue.

Soon, there were four adults working on removing his chubby finger from this rocking chair while I held back the giggles. *This stuff only happens to you,* I told myself. I managed to keep all his little friends occupied while four adults carried him out of the room to the nurse's office. One supporting his hand, two carrying him, and one carrying the chair where the nurse managed to remove his finger rather quickly. He returned with an age-old cure to all elementary school ailments: the paper towel "ice pack."

The lesson continued, followed by an offer of employment. I was thrilled. It was another dream come true and I couldn't have been happier. I knew it was going to be challenging but I also knew I was meant to be here.

I attended spring parent-teacher conferences the following week and completed all my orientation at Human Resources in downtown St. Louis. I had my employee badge, keys to my classroom, and benefits package. My start date was March 23, 2020. The day the world shut down. The day we thought that time could be paused like the sands of time in an hourglass and the world would turn back to the way it was.

A week later when schools decided to try virtual learning, my new principal and I had begun planning for me to launch a virtual classroom. I had been collaborating with my new teammates and while I knew it would be a challenge to establish relationships with these little learners, it was something I was excited about trying. I had visions of taking books and resources to my new families and new Sparkling Scholars. I was ready to go except that HR hadn't issued my online passwords, accounts, or email address. I couldn't do my job without those components, so I called them to determine what the hold-up was.

"You never physically reported for work prior to the 23rd. You needed to physically report for work," was the standard human resources response.

"I went in for parent teacher conferences. I *couldn't* go to work; it was spring break, and my planned start date was this past Monday." I said firmly.

"Ma'am, I'm sorry. We don't have a record of your presence so we can't add you to the payroll." She was unyielding.

"I have a key card, I have completed my orientation, and have my employee identification number though," I bargained.

"I'm sorry, there is nothing we can do."

"But I don't understand. This situation is unprecedented. My families and students deserve a teacher, not a substitute teacher. These children have already been through enough, they deserve a qualified, highly effective teacher that can help ensure they don't develop more gaps in their learning." I was confused.

"You need to physically scan your card and report for work in order to be employed and get paid." Her response was formulated and robotic. She hung up. I was dumbfounded and yet I wasn't all at once. St. Louis Public Schools didn't come by their notorious reputation over nothing. Here was a passionate teacher who was begging them to let her fill one of the empty positions that they had significant trouble filling prior to pandemic woes. Still, the fact that their human resources department was splitting hairs over semantics when a principal, families, coworkers, and most importantly students wanted an effective, vivacious teacher on their staff was insanity. To refuse a teacher to work with families that she had met during parent teacher conferences, highlighted the brokenness of the system.

All she wanted was to ensure her little kindergarteners would not fall behind more than their insurmountable odds had already thrown at them. It was infuriating that a district that served a mostly African American population, during the inception of a national pandemic, lacked any code of ethics. They were aiding and abetting the failure of minority students in an underfunded, underprivileged school. They didn't care about what the administrators in the buildings wanted, the Central office only cared about a scan card and flexing their muscle by cutting the administration's knees out from underneath them.

Tragically, that sweet class didn't have a certified teacher the remainder of that year. They were going to need one if they were going to learn to read. It was this single incident that taught me about the public school system and how broken it was, always protecting the bottom line over the lives of the people they claimed to care about. I walked away disillusioned because I had wanted nothing more than to walk in and make a difference in the lives of my students.

As it was, I needed a key card to do that and an official time-stamped clock-in for work. As the saying goes, the path to hell is paved with good intentions. I'd add, money is the asphalt that gets you there. Follow the money, you'll find the corruption.

WHEN SCHOOLS FAIL

"Education is the most powerful weapon you can use to change the world."
-Nelson Mandela

I never fully got over the disillusionment with the public-school systems after that. I went into the fall of that year, responding to the whisper to teach yet again. The desire in my heart to work with kids and have an impact on their lives never left me. It was as much a part of me as the rhythm of my heartbeat. I couldn't separate my love of teaching and working with kids any more than I could write without my left hand. It just was. I knew I needed to honor that calling, even if it meant the unraveling of me, like a row of crochet when you pull on the end of the yarn.

I went into the fall, with Covid in full swing, hired on as a special education teacher in a district that serves students with special needs. It was a definite career move-I was getting my master's in educational administration and the position offered to me was one where I would oversee multiple teacher's assistants, write performance evaluations, and ensure that student's Individual Education Plans, or IEPs, were written and followed. It was a big job and required me to be cognizant and ethical with adhering to federal guidelines.

I had to make sure that learning was differentiated to meet the needs of my students, that collaboration was happening with classroom teachers, ensuring that behavior plans were implemented and followed correctly...all while doing it online. On Zoom.

When I was hired, it was made very clear to me, both in my written contract and by my administrator that I was a resource room teacher, which was an ideal position for a special educator. I was excited to be able to collaborate with classroom teachers, to adjust what they were teaching to meet the individual needs of my students who had different learning abilities. This was something that I did as a general classroom teacher and excelled in. I was excited to be able to be successful at this new role, even if it was virtual. With the support of other teachers, I was confident that this could be done.

In reality, I was lied to in their attempt to fill a slot. A week into my new role, I was sharing my ideas with my teacher assistants and my vision for what their role would look like in supporting our students. They had been with our caseload of students last year and were well familiar with their unique needs. They looked at me like I was some version of Medusa.

"These kids are self-contained." My young teacher assistant told me, patiently.

"What? I was told I was hired as a resource room teacher."

"These kids are definitely self-contained," Kandace said again.

She went on to tell me more about the students on our roster and outlined their needs and abilities. It was clear that these students were self-contained.

After my initial shock wore off, I approached my administrator and asked him. "Oh, yeah, yeah, yeah. Right. That's correct, you are a self-contained teacher."

With school slated to start, I had three days to pivot what I had been told and change my entire plan. I definitely would not have signed up to teach a self-contained classroom, especially with a classroom that contained extreme behaviors. To be frank, who would? These rooms are notorious for no support, burn out, and being assaulted daily. Regardless, I felt God calling me to stay here and serve in this role. I was determined to learn all I could and to use this experience to help strengthen me as a teacher.

The first day of virtual school started and it was obvious it was going to be a cluster- of something- from that first day. The district expected us to meet every single IEP as it was written for in person learning but failed to modify or adapt it for a virtual learning model. Every minute of every IEP of my students on my caseload needed to be met, virtually, even though their plan was written for in person learning. I had ten years of experience prior to this in the classroom and yet I felt completely unprepared and unsupported.

My students and their families were depending on me to help them navigate this year and uphold their learning plans, but it was impossible to do on Zoom. My students ranged from extreme autism, cerebral palsy, oppositional defiant disorder, extreme ADHD, and anything in between. I was expected to keep them engaged for six hours a day, on Zoom. We were not to give breaks and we were to keep them logged on for that long, calling parents when a student didn't return from a break, turned the camera off, or muted themselves.

The idea that the structure couldn't bend to apply the salve of grace to families with special needs kids, or the teachers who were trying desperately to figure out how to make this virtual stress mess work was bothersome. When a structure fails to serve the people it claims to benefit, and instead creates undue stress and anxiety on the backs of those receiving services or giving them- it's clear that reform is needed.

I knew that what was happening was a grave injustice. These children needed to have in-person learning, but that wasn't an option. Staring at a screen, with an adult or older sibling next to you to fill in the role that the teacher's assistants had played wasn't serving anyone. It was an injustice because rather than learn, these students, who already struggled, were becoming burnt out. Daily I could see their fires die, and I felt it inside me too. I knew we were failing these kids, yet I met them on Zoom every morning ready to do what was asked of me in the name of helping kids.

Except I knew deep down I wasn't.

My oldest had developed a significant drug and substance abuse disorder. I felt woefully ill-equipped to handle his complex brain, let alone the complex brains of my students. Teaching, and having a personal crisis were proving to be incompatible partnerships. I never dreamt after the life I had lived that I would be facing a serious crisis of my own.

Here I was, teaching in a pandemic, in a district whose demands were impossible to meet, as a single mom.

My oldest, was experiencing the impact that months of isolation will do to you when you desire connection, have a family history of drug usage and chemical dependency, and have higher-functioning autism.

My son began to require 24-hour care. He would use during the day when I was at work, when I arrived home he would be in the middle of a "bad trip" threatening suicide and having extreme anxiety throughout the evening, which prevented me from rest at night. I had a job to maintain and a son to keep alive. This was a crisis exacerbated by Covid. My own children always came first, and I would absolutely ensure that I did everything in my power to put my son first now. Surely my district would approve my request for FMLA. They knew that my son had autism and that he was the reason why I wanted to go into special education. I sent in my request for FMLA.

I gained all of the documentation I needed from the hospital I had to take Noah to, his therapist, and his pediatrician who all cited the need for Noah to be provided 24-hour care. This crisis was prohibiting me from effectively doing my job for an undetermined amount of time. I had no idea how long this long, dark night would last, but I knew that my own special needs son had to come before anyone else's.

My request was denied. Denied because, similar to St. Louis Public Schools where the district has a disconnect to what is actually transpiring within the schools and the people who work there, I hadn't worked there long enough to qualify for leave.

I was infuriated. *Really?! So, if I had a car wreck and was incapacitated for a time, I wouldn't qualify because I hadn't worked here long enough?* I was over it all.

I went back and forth with human resources for about a week. Denied. Denied. Denied.

I sent my resignation letter, knowing the professional risks to myself but my own son's life was on the line. Breaking generational strongholds and generations of substance abuse is not for the weak. This was a battle I knew that I had to fight, even if it meant great personal cost to myself.

To Whom it May Concern:

This is a letter I never imagined I would be in a position to be writing: Covid has not been kind. I am writing today to issue my formal resignation and inform you that I am leaving the teaching profession. Earlier this month, my oldest son, a senior in high school and also a special needs student with autism, was diagnosed with substance abuse issues. After picking him up at his father's house, it was apparent that he was alarmingly high on some controlled substance, and I immediately took him to his therapist. Together, we determined that the next course of action was to take him to the ER. He now requires around the clock monitoring.

I am a single mom and the demands and pull of teaching are too great for me at this time to continue to give my students what they need and deserve in the classroom: an engaged, caring, present, and dedicated teacher. My priorities at this time dictate that I must place and value my own boys above my career. Due to the fact that I have not been employed for longer than a year, I do not have the option to take FMLA. Thank you for giving me the opportunity to serve.

Respectfully,
Chandra Hawkins

The system chose to exercise its power over the success of its students. They refused to accept my resignation. I, like David, found myself unwittingly engaged in a war with Goliath on a professional and personal level.

I had become completely disillusioned with the toxic structure of administration within public schools. It was obvious to me that the needs of the system were elevated over the actual, realized needs of teachers and students. It was no longer a system that worked. Sure, I had seen issues in the public schools before; issues like the need for a healthy evaluation process, issues with collaboration, data collection, and testing but to not be able to bend when a teacher was having a traumatic personal crisis and allow her job to remain intact when it was a legally protected status under FMLA blew my "pea-pickin' heart," as Mamo would have said.

I felt like my story, my journey in education wasn't complete. I didn't know why, but I felt God calling me to try one last time to leave an impact and also be taught lessons I might not yet know. Pandemic learning had become sadly, tragically, almost normalized the following school year. We all knew that was a lie. Teachers everywhere were bemoaning the fact that what we were being asked to do wasn't helping our students with what they truly needed, mentally, emotionally, or academically. The system continues to ask teachers to do the impossible with no support and precious little pay. No one feels those factors perhaps more keenly than a single parent.

I knew, as I said earlier, that my story wasn't done. And again, I couldn't place my finger on it, but I was determined to follow God's call and pursued teaching in a Christian private school. This school was a school that I had grown up hearing about and my childhood church home supported. I felt that gaining experience within a private school would help broaden my perspective on education at large.

I felt that teaching in a private school would help me to clearly compare and contrast and perhaps revitalize my understanding and appreciation of schools. Christian schools had the opportunity to apply grace, healing, and restoration when done correctly. I was hoping my disillusionment would improve. And it didn't.

At first, this school appeared to be a beacon of hope to lower income, African American families who wanted their child to attend there. I was told over and over again how diverse this school was and what a blessing it was to see people walking in diversity, from all different backgrounds, side by side living out our faith journeys.

I was so excited. I honestly and openly shared about my passion for Black Lives Matter, my dedication to working with students, and the journey I had taken to help me recognize the importance that a teacher has on the lives of their students in the interview process. I felt like at long last, I was home. I was thrilled to be teaching sixth grade literacy and to be able to use literature that would bring us together, just like I had done when I taught third grade several years ago.

Nothing could have prepared me for the bullying of white, wealthy parents who didn't want their kids around a woke white Christian teacher or a black student body. I had students taking notes on everything I said. I was censored. The longer I taught here, the more racism I saw. Affluent, white Protestant parents didn't like the way the black families were, they felt, preferred. There was a complete lack of empathy on the part of the white familial demographic, and they were not afraid to rock the boat and go to the board to exert their power to get their way. After all, their money wielded an incredible level of power. Teachers were seen as the enemy and were made to do whatever the affluent, white families wanted because they were the ones who had the money funding the school. It was literally like teaching without any personal integrity. I had to go in, be a doormat, be quiet and submissive, and look the part of the good, white, Christian school girl.

I had come too far to let anyone do that to me ever again. I wasn't about to tolerate their racism and I wasn't going to play their games to save face. It was a toxic work environment where parents ran the show and were bullies to teachers in the name of loving Jesus. Administrators abetted the bullying on behalf of the parents. If they didn't it meant those parents could just walk away and pay tuition elsewhere. There was no support for teachers from administration. They didn't have our backs; they had the backs of the parents.

And in that moment I realized that school in all forms as we know it, had failed.

THE NEED FOR REFORM

"Learning is about so much more than just filling in the right bubble."
-President Barack Obama

After fifty years of growing together, raising their kids, and watching their grandkids grow up, the time had come for Mamo and Granddad to sell the family farm and move into town. One of the most painful things our family did was to sort through fifty years of memories. Alzheimer's disease had ravaged Mamo's once crystalline memory and left us on the other side of it, longing to see remnants of hope that she remembered the fascinating life she had lived. She had such a beautiful life, and her journals were impeccable recollections of the daily things that made up her life and left us a glimpse into a bygone era. Her childhood was spent during the Great Depression. She watched as her family had been homesteaders in Montana and had to sell their claim to come back to Fairfax to save the family farm after her Grandpa had died. She never forgot scarcity. Her anecdote to this fear was to save everything, which was overwhelming when the time came to sort through the belongings and sentimental keepsakes of five decades of a life well-lived.

I remember finding this old, tattered box in one of the piles brought down from the spare bedroom that was never used, except for storage. It had bizarre, faded lettering on the sides in shades of honey mustard and dusty blue jeans. I wiped off the dust that was caked to the top.

You never knew what you were going to find when you opened a box, some boxes held vestiges of memories from the past, some were filled with inconsequential things like old aluminum foil. You never knew. I thought this one would be a good find, since it was upstairs, hidden behind my Aunt's vintage troll doll collection and it was heavy.

I lifted the lid. As I opened it, I could smell the dusty pages of forgotten books and magazines, like smelling the comforting scents of an old bookstore, burnt coffee, and mustiness from pages that have sat too long. I peered into the box. It was like catching a scene from a part of Mamo's life that I wished I had talked to her more about. Everything was just as she left it. Pictures were drawn on brittle, yellowed paper in varied handwriting and styles. *To Miss McGinnis, Love, Tommy. To Miss McGinnis, Love, Jeanie Barrett. To Miss McGinnis, Thank you for helping me with the Christmas pageant. Yours Truly, Christopher Brown.* Picture after picture, floated to the ground as I sent them to the floor from the edge of the bed. Some letters were faded, discolored, some ripped from years of wear. Underneath these delicate pictures, a stack of magazines. *The Grade Teacher,* April 1949. *The Grade Teacher,* May 1949. *The Grade Teacher,* September 1948. Spines and covers still intact, I was curious. I was nineteen and thinking about the promise of my future.

My mind drifted to the conversation we had around the dining room table years before, almost as if the table that was just around the corner was whispering to me...*I always thought you'd be a teacher someday...*I flipped through the pages. There were graphs for epic chalkboard bulletin boards with how-to steps on creating a beautiful design on your chalkboard. Beautiful, but I shuddered at the thought of picking up a piece of chalk and drawing on one myself. Advertisements in the magazines were for typewriters, chalk, pencils. Hidden beneath this dusty, brittle pile of yellowed papers and magazines lay hidden a stack of very old books. They were tan and Bloody Mary red with beautiful gold leaf on the spines. *Public School Methods, Project Edition, 1927.* Three books, Volumes one, four, and six. They beckoned me to peruse their fragile pages.

I was mesmerized. Hundreds of pages of college textbook material that Mamo had read and used when she earned her teaching certificate. Some sections were earmarked. Tenderly, I noticed she had placed tiny pieces of lined paper for places to return to. There was a placemark on a picture of Yellowstone National Park, a dream of hers to go and travel to. She always spoke of Montana and how much she loved the place of her early childhood. She didn't know it when she marked this spot in the book that someday the dream she had when she was twenty would come true for her.

Granddad would make that dream come true for her just a few years after they had met on their honeymoon. There were other spots where she had left lined pieces of notebook paper to help her remember to tell her students about her love of birds and geese. She told me she loved birds because they were free. Tears fell down my cheeks, splashing the pages of the textbook I was holding. She didn't remember the beautiful life she had anymore. I gathered this box and placed it in my car. I knew these things were important to me because of what her and I had shared. I knew I needed to hold on to them and I felt like Mary, who pondered treasured things in her heart.

That moment proved to be more pivotal than I had initially given it credit for. It was in that moment, flipping through my grandmother's passages of time and teaching, that I became inspired. Her students loved her, she loved what she did, and the impact she had was clear. She loved everything about her one-room schoolhouse, Cherry Dale, and ensured that the memories of it were preserved. I wanted that kind of life. That moment watered the seed that had been planted just a few short years ago when we sat around the dining room table, and she had asked me what I wanted to do when I was done with school. Somehow, someday, I was going to be like Mamo when I grew up.

Mamo taught at the height of the emergence of educational theories. Her textbooks were clearly constructivist* in theory, a methodology formalized by the theorist John Piaget. These textbooks also reflected another profound theorist who has shaped our view of education for the last hundred years, John Dewey. His hands-on approach to learning was apparent throughout the pages of this book.

Page after page, section after section, these textbooks, *Public School Methods,* which helped shape a generation of teachers and learners, contained example after example of practical ideas on how to teach math, science, reading, drama, poetry, and geography. The activities were engaging and student-centered, reflecting the thoughts and trends of the time. Teachers were encouraged and allowed to create test questions that they felt were markers of student understanding and were given suggestions of lessons with possible outlines, but it was evident that they were not micromanaged. I was struck by a section of *Public-School Methods, Volume 4*:

Difficult as it is to give in print an example of a good lesson, we print one here, with the expressed understanding that there is probably no teacher who will give the lesson on exactly this plan and no class to which it is adapted just as it stands. Yet the plan and its execution are both good and ought to be eminently suggestive to every live teacher.

When I was in the classroom, rarely did I or any teacher have this level of trust and autonomy. We were told regularly what to teach and how to teach it. Teachers that I taught with that approached education like myself, used a backwards design* concept, unpacked state standards, and then adapted current research, theories, and curriculum to fit our students' needs. We often found ourselves in an uphill battle where we were being asked to implement a scripted* curriculum.

These curricula are ironically published by the largest educational publishing companies and whose assessments, perhaps even more ironically, mirrored both state standardized tests and had questions that were grade-level appropriate but also mirrored college preparatory exams.

As teachers, we generally hated scripted curriculums. When they were rolled out and presented, usually replacing a curriculum that required far more involvement on the part of teachers, the professional development room would heave a collective, silent groan. It killed our autonomy, creativity, and insulted our intelligence to be told our scores weren't good enough or that we weren't doing enough to ensure student success. We wanted to be trusted that we knew how to ask questions and teach content in ways that students could learn. The approach of using a packaged, scripted curriculum was a magic bullet of sorts, the district felt. No one ever questioned if the student achievement outcomes we were looking for were realistic. No one ever questioned if the standardized assessments we were using were unbiased or effective. No. It was an accepted fact that standardized assessments were a thing and that the way these assessments were formatted and presented to students was par for the course.

The longer I taught, the more I witnessed and began to wonder. The curriculum and resources that we were asked to use, whether a scripted resource or not, were all published under one of the major educational publishing houses, Houghton-Mifflin, Pearson Education, McGraw-Hill, or Heinemann Publishing. These publishing houses are responsible for the educational content that drives student instruction in classrooms today.

Their sales representatives would present their product to Superintendents of Curriculum and Instruction or principals at educational conferences or sometimes in person at our district and pitch "why" their curriculum met our student's needs. Promises would be made that if this curriculum was used with fidelity (which was a fancy way of saying, one size fits all), then student scores would rise, and it would benefit the district because they could garner an increase in funding.

It didn't matter what school I was a part of teachers spanned a wide variety of backgrounds and approaches to student learning, yet we were all successful at helping our students meet the mark regardless of our personal style (as long as that style of teaching was rooted in kindness). However, when a district made a decision to roll out a new curriculum that "everyone needed to use," there would be push-back from us. Why resist something your administrators wanted you to do? Simply put because we weren't consulted. Our feedback was rarely considered, and if it was, it was limited. Perhaps we would have a choice of a few options (ironically our options would only ever be a choice from one of the leading educational publishing houses), however, the choice to formulate and consider something completely new or synthesized to meet our student demographics was not considered. The curriculum resource would be purchased, costing taxpayers and our district thousands of dollars. We would be told to throw out the old curriculum, ensuring we only had the new, costly resource to use.

Using teacher created resources such as elements found on a widely popular teacher website, Teachers Pay

Teachers, was strongly discouraged and sometimes banned. I began to ask why.

Why would our voices not matter? We were the ones that were ensuring that our students had what they needed. We cared deeply about kids and their success, or we wouldn't have been in this work. It was a calling for each and every professional I had the privilege of working with. Gone were the days where teachers went into this field for the summers off or to take a nap on the couch in the teachers' lounge. We were in this work because we loved kids and wanted to touch young lives. Granted, there were always a handful who needed accountability, but that was not the majority. That was not those of us who, like me, were asked to serve on leadership teams and literacy teams, seeking our input on new curriculum because we were strong, capable, effective teachers. At the end of the day, we simply weren't trusted to have a voice. Sure, we could give input on which selection the district should purchase, but doing the research on our own, finding curriculum options we wanted to use apart from district input, was not something that occurred in the school districts I worked in. The educational companies, with their research, glossy pamphlets, and lofty promises of raising student test scores should their curricular resources be purchased, were. Their choices were displayed, with their curriculum representatives dressed in business attire, while we would look at the overwhelming options in our school tee-shirts. Ask any teacher if they feel confident to make a decision that will affect their students and coworkers' professional lives and well-being, after writing detailed sub plans the night before, just to be pulled out for half a day. It's hard to feel good about your decision and to feel that your voice matters when you're given only a few hours in a high-pressured setting to do so.

The art of making high-pressured decisions under imposed time constraints was something I was all too familiar with. My ex had subjected me to years of that. This smelled familiar, all too familiar. It felt toxic. To be told you must make a decision using a resource that tells you how to do your job and to do so under a high-pressure environment is unhealthy. I began to consider if other professionals from other professions would tolerate their bosses coming in and laying out exactly how they should conduct their day-to-day assignments and work-related goals. Would they tolerate such blatant disrespect?

The pressure to test students using the benchmark assessments that came as a part of the package of the district's chosen curriculum mounted. When I administered the Missouri State's MAP test, a test that all 3rd-8th grade students are required to take as a part of Every Student Succeeds Act, (The act was passed in December 2015 under President Obama), it was obvious that the *Wonders* curriculum and accompanying tests were mirror images of our state test. The types of questions, the structure, and components were all the same.

The more consistently we used our *Wonders* tests, the better our students would score on the state test. The higher the scores on the state test, the more money our school would get from the federal government.

This is a striking departure from the methodology of 1929 America, where testing was actually considered "questioning" and a far cry from the business that testing has clearly become.

Questioning may go too far, and in the effort to create interest the teacher may kill it. She must be wide-awake, ready to change to something else at the right moment.
-Public School Methods, Volume 4

My thoughts exactly. Questioning can go too far. Sometimes, information takes time to process. Sometimes, information doesn't require a response. Occasionally, when I was giving a test or administering a reading level assessment, I wanted to ask a question in a different way. I wanted that freedom to "change something else at the right moment." As it was, if I wanted my data to count and not be biased, I had to administer the assessment as it was written. It pained me, because sometimes the questions on the tests used words that weren't developmentally or culturally appropriate. I was struck with the impact of how assessments that weren't written for kids in lower socio-economic statuses, or kids whose environment used different wording, when I was administering a reading assessment to one of my first graders. One of the questions centered around a word choice that this reading program had determined was appropriate to use based on the level. This directly impacted this student's outcomes.

Romero had a rough homelife. His dad was in and out of the home, and his mom was a hard-working single mom who worked third shift. His pants were often up to his calves and his shoes were frequently falling apart. It was springtime, and that meant we were finalizing reading levels for the upcoming year. I knew he could read, and I knew he was capable of being above grade level in reading. The way this program worked was he needed to pass a level before I could move him up, much like a ladder. I couldn't skip a rung; each level was important to achieving the next step higher. The expectation was that he would be at an emerging second-grade reading level by the end of first grade in May. He was currently just below grade level, and I was determining if he could move higher. I continued to feel confident as we approached the deadline that when we were done, I would be able to move him within a stone's throw to the level he would need to be at for second grade.

The program was asking him to read a short, illustrated book that he had never before seen or had read to him. It was a story about a little boy who had lost an object and needed help finding it. The house in this text looked nothing like his, I was certain. On every page was a picture of a different room in the house with different pieces of furniture that you would expect to find in an upper-middle class, generally white suburban home. The text was predictable, until you got to the piece of furniture featured on the pages, which was intentional because the student needed to use their understanding of phonics to determine how to correctly sound out the given word. The little boy in the short story went and looked behind a shelf, an ottoman, a couch, and a table for the missing picture that he wanted to give to his teacher. Part of the consideration of reading level placement on the part of the teacher is the crucial retelling of a story, from the beginning to the end as well as being able to answer questions about the text. You are looking for a student to use keywords, the power of recall, and an overall understanding of what occurred in the story.

Romero failed that level. He failed because in his entire short life, he had never seen an ottoman. He may have had a footstool in his home, or at least knew what that was, but the book used the word ottoman. He also had no idea what a couch was because he called it a sofa. He wasn't able to comprehend the text, or accurately answer the questions because this house didn't look like his, and the words used in the text didn't reflect his culture. He went into second grade marked behind level, because I couldn't move him up a rung on the reading ladder. He wasn't the only one.

Why educational publishing houses think tricking kids is a component of good, healthy education, I will never know or attempt to understand. This was a tragedy. Romero was a young, black male living below the poverty line. He was identified from the age of first grade as being a student who needed intervention, because he wasn't able to identify with the culture that was depicted in the pages of a book that a publishing house said was a mark of reading comprehension. Romero didn't have a problem reading. He had a problem performing. He had a problem performing to upper-middle class standards. My fear was that he would carry the narrative that he was "behind grade level" with him into other grades. My fear was that that he would shut down and believe he was incapable of learning or feeling confident in his reading abilities.

The narrative that was destined to follow him from a young age was that he was identified as needing reading remediation, and it wasn't even true! The fear is that boys and girls like my Romero would grow up believing the lies that they weren't good readers, or that they were falling short of a standard that wasn't fair to begin with. This is an injustice. My eyes began to open for the need for an educational reformation.

Constructivism is a theory of learning that states, simply, that children learn best through the construction of using different senses, inputs, and stimuli to construct their knowledge. It also theorizes that children learn best in classrooms that are student centered, or student directed.

Backward design is a method of planning where teachers look at where a student needs to be in relation to an objective. Then, using that as a starting point, they intentionally prepare lessons that are broken down into measurable steps in order for students to achieve the desired result.

Scripted curriculum is a curriculum where teachers are explicitly told exactly what to say, how to say it, what questions to ask, and exactly what resources to use. The expectation from districts who adopt these resources are that teachers will use them with "fidelity" which means, as they are written, that all students in the school are getting the same instruction regardless of teacher or teacher knowledge/ability/specialty.

RACIALLY BIASED PRACTICES

"I see it like global warming. We have a serious problem that requires big, structural changes; otherwise, we are dooming future generations to catastrophe. Our inability to think structurally, with a sense of mutual care, is dooming us — whether the problem is racism, or climate disaster, or world peace."
- Mari J. Matsuda

What will it take to be courageous and step into the difficult, unknown? One would have thought that the wokeness that emerged from our 2020 collective rally from the murders of George Floyd and Breonna Taylor would have been enough to illicit discussions about how deeply we need the salve of grace and healing to be applied to our systems where injustice reigns. One would have thought that if anything would have shaken, woke, and broken our educational, legal, justice, and economic systems up that that would have been the catalyst for such reform.

Granted, it perhaps nudged the dial closer. Increased numbers of white people, and in particular educators, have been receptive to honestly evaluating racial bias and doing what they can to change that which is within their sphere of influence.

More books were written and read, more conversations had, more white allies emerged, more risks taken with bold conversations. But it's too far from actual, impactful change. For every step we take forward, there are grassroots movements that actively combat allies who are working to thwart systemic change from behind the scenes.

Behind the passage of laws that legalized homeschooling that were passed in the 1980's through various state legislatures, was a movement that learned the power of lobbying. This movement became a grassroots movement that espoused conservative values, reduced governmental intrusion, and protecting laws that upheld religious and political liberties. This movement was composed of parents who wanted homeschooling legalized. They learned the power of calling state representatives and voicing their concerns, writing letters, directly meeting state representatives so they knew your face when you called, and "shutting down" the operator board at the state capitol.

I was eight when we made my first trip to our state capital. We were told to wear our Sunday best and were coached on how to shake hands, make eye contact, and be on our best behavior. Our purpose was to voice concerns for a law that would require an added layer of accountability for homeschoolers. We wanted the current Missouri law (the same one that is still in place today) to remain untouched. What better way to voice our opposition than to show up to your local state representatives office than with your small children and home-baked goodies to sweeten the deal? Something akin to the old saying, "You catch more flies with honey than vinegar."

This was the first of annual trips I would take to the Jefferson City capitol building. In the years that followed, I would become a spokesperson, shaking hands with state representatives, and telling them what I claimed I wanted. I would pass out letters I had written to their secretaries stating why homeschool freedoms were important. I would wait to meet with state senators, sometimes being allowed to interrupt committees as these powerful men who held my fate in their hands began to know who my family was. It was thrilling in a way, to know the Capitol building in all its grandeur, with all the familiarity of my Grandma's house. I knew how to get to the floor of either chamber. I learned the appropriate way to wait to be introduced as a special guest. I knew what it was to sit in the guest chambers of the state senate. I had learned through my parents the value and inner workings of state government. Because our state representatives and senators knew us, whenever a call was placed to voice concerns over any possible piece of legislation that would have infringed on homeschooler's freedoms (which generally were increased accountability measures to ensure homeschool students had an adequate education and to prevent educational neglect), it took no more than a handful of phone calls from constituents for their vote to be influenced. The power we wielded because we were willing to meet them personally and create a presence in our State Capitol was undeniable.

Influence. It's what The Movement wanted and sought after. The Movement wanted unrestrained control to make government and laws suit our needs. They might not have wanted to hold office themselves (although several of our homeschooling fathers did do so eventually) but they *were* willing to do whatever it took to create that influence. What better way to have direct influence on government and to ensure your agenda is adhered to than to work a campaign. When manpower is short, and campaign money is tight, having devoted campaign workers who can work any hours of the day, for free, is an asset especially if you have political aspirations.

Our parents would promise to have our family work their campaigns, keeping track of our homeschool lesson hours under "Government" or "History," in exchange for the promise that the state representative or senator would protect homeschool freedoms. I was ten when I went on my first canvassing, following a grid of homes to pass fliers and political brochures out too. I was twelve when I began cold calling, spending hours into the night at local campaign offices asking strangers on the phone for votes for candidates that I would not be able to vote for until I was eighteen. I dealt with crabby, mean, old men who asked how old I was and people hanging up clearly annoyed at the little girl's voice on the other end of the line. Sometimes, I got thanked for my service and devotion to our country. As I became a teenager, I grew to love the rush of campaign season. I loved working the polls or cold calling asking for votes. I loved the rush of tracking voter data, feeling that I was making an impact.

I worked for John Ashcroft and President George W. Bush, U.S. Senator Kit Bond, U.S. Congressman Todd Akin, and a host of other presidential candidates throughout the years. I was working my way up in the political scene and it was exhilarating. All in the name of freedom.

In that same name of freedom today, garnered by the same energy that drove our Movement in the 1990's, is the same type of grassroots movement where parents are showing up to school board meetings. These parents have learned that if they voice their concerns, are seen and recognized by people who possess a certain level of power, that they can yield a similar form of power.

These parents are the same ones that are driving educational decisions in a broad sense today, parents who want their kids in public school because of the affordability, or any other myriad of reasons why families make decisions that they feel are in their child's best interests. There are parents who show up to school board meetings demanding that school districts revisit their health policies. Parents who don't want sex education taught or their child's personal freedom infringed on by wearing a mask. Parents who know how to work their state government and lobby for bills that will ensure that critical race theory (CRT) is not taught or discussed. Parents who want a year's worth of lesson plans submitted to a committee who will censor and approve what a teacher can teach.

Teachers are bullied, harassing emails sent, school administrators coerced into appeasing parents that they feel obligated to oblige. Those that disagree are drug along by the voices of the clamoring crowd and don't feel safe enough to express their dissention.

How did we arrive at the point where we can no longer have civil discourse and discuss the hard things? For centuries, this has marked educational and philosophical systems. Ancient philosophers such as Socrates, the Apostle Paul, and others have eloquently debated, defended, and engaged in civil discourse over their own beliefs, even while doing so passionately. When groups begin to suggest that they cannot listen to another's side because they feel threatened with the existence of their premise, no matter what that belief or premise is, this is the downfall of thought and civilization. Yet this is the crux of where we are.

Stakeholders in education have politicized topics regarding humanity and race. Topics that should stem from our mutual love of fellow mankind and empathy to hear another's perspective are "shushed" and glossed over. Hard topics like racially biased practices in education have gone largely unchallenged and discussed, leading to a vacuum of silence where a vocal minority have risen to fill in the void- demanding that CRT or any discussions regarding social justice cease. Students can use racial slurs, hate speech, and express racism openly and walk away with little more than an out of school suspension. Our students of color see the lack of realized justice when they witness a classmate expressing these vitriolic slurs and return the next day, having little more than a hand slap with a wet noodle.

It is the lack of firm responses to these behaviors on the part of school administration that has led to situations like the tragedy we witnessed in Buffalo, NY in 2022 where an 18-year-old white male thinks it is somehow his duty to commit the worst racial massacre in recent history. Schools are afraid to label evil actions as evil.

It's time for a strong rebuttal.

I was wrapping up my master's degree, in educational leadership, that summer of 2020. So much had transpired that year, and just months prior, I was starkly confronted with the opportunity to take a bold stance for Black Lives Matter once again. I didn't know what I was going to write my master's thesis on when I signed up for my capstone class. I began to gather ideas and then promptly discarded them as the events began to unfold from that summer.

I began to ask myself, what would it look like if racism was addressed in schools? Historically, schools have been looked to as institutions that prepare and train the next generation. I began to understand that confronting racism needed to begin with the schools. Children learn racism from seeing it modeled or overtly spoken about in their homes or the silence and abdication of hard conversations growing up. What I wasn't prepared for was the depth of how racist our school system is and remains today.

When the Columbine High School shooting happened, just a month before I graduated high school in April of 1999, it changed the way that school is operated by ushering in a wave of legislation called the Safe Schools Act. This legislative approach sought to address school violence and gave parameters to administrators and educators on handling discipline issues such as bullying, weapons on the premises, and drug usage. While each state has their own unique legislation on this topic, what remains universal is the umbrella of student discipline that is contained within each law.

Arguably, the need for such legislation and discussions around how to keep all schools safe were needed to prevent such horrors as what happened at Columbine High School or Sandy Hook Elementary School. What was not addressed was how teachers, traditionally middle-class white females, would address their own bias to ensure that there was equity in the request for discipline should a student be deemed as needing it. The subjective nature of discipline within the variance of cultural context and dynamics has led to the improper identification of so-called behavioral concerns, particularly amongst black students. Black students in schools across America will tell you that they are given stricter disciplinary consequences than their white peers for the same offense. The data supports this, and I used it in my research project titled, *Impacts of Racial Bias in Educational Practices:*

The zero-tolerance discipline policies that many schools continue to use has given rise to academic scholars researching the rise of OSS and ISS among students and its connection to our criminal justice system. This trend has now been termed the School-to-Prison-Pipeline. Students of color who are expelled and suspended from school have an alarming connection to later forming a connection to juvenile delinquency and time served in our prison system (Delate-O'Conner, Alvarez, Murray,

Milner, 2017; Morris, 2016; Moody, 2016; Alexander, 2010). Young black males make up about 8% of the nation's public-school students but have 37% of Out of School Suspensions and In School Suspensions assigned to them (Carter, 2019).

White teachers tend to refer white students for objective offenses that are definable and easily proven through due process, whereas students of color tend to be referred to the office for subjective offenses that are more ambiguous and not as easily proven, leading to a systemic injustice issue (Delate-O'Conner, Alvarez, Murray, Milner; 2017).

The more I dug, the more I witnessed the stark realities of the School-to-Prison Pipeline. Policies like dress codes found in student handbooks. Students are found to have infractions for hair that is deemed distracting to the learning environment, or young people are told that they can't wear hoodies with the hood over their head. What is poorly understood, is the cultural reason why young black students enjoy wearing hoodies. This is a cultural difference that should be honored. Teachers rarely question if a young person wears attire favoring Billie Eilish but would question a young person wearing attire that would favor Nelly or Young Dolph; due to their own biases that are supported by unfair school policies.

Consequently, this perpetuates a white consciousness and racist view that says if you see a young black person wearing a hoodie on the street, trouble may be present because to wear a hoodie in school is akin to wearing a face covering. These policies have historically been assigned to keep students faces unobstructed due to the fact that the shooters of Columbine (and other weaponized massacre-ists since then) wore face masks for at least a portion of the shooting. Others have worn gas masks and ski masks since then. The reasoning is that to maintain school safety we must require faces to be easily identified. And yet we somehow made massive allowances to this rule during the Covid-19 pandemic. Our school's practices are still, in 2022, based largely on disciplinary policies that have the capacity to be used to keep black students in check by school staff who have their own racial bias. These policies maintain a collective fear of people of color while preserving socially accepted norms of white middle-class America.

Teachers use tactics throughout their classrooms to help maintain an orderly learning environment. One of the techniques I learned was simple little chants to get student attention but to quiet down a noisy room. Some of these are the traditional call-and-response models with fun sayings where I might have said, "Macaroni and cheese!" To which, my scholars would reply, "Everybody freeze!" Rooms can get quite busy, and they bustle with the activity of learning. Sometimes there is a lot of energy contained in one room! It is helpful to have an easy way to grab the attention of bustling learners. When I was researching racially biased practices in education, it was obvious that so many teachers didn't understand the origin of this classroom management technique. One such simple technique that I used to get little people to quiet down so they could hear my instruction was to tell my Sparkling Scholars to, "Catch a bubble!" In which, fifteen little people would collectively swallow or gulp a mouthful of air and contain within their cheeks, air bubbles. Wide eyed, looking at me, with little chipmunk cheeks. It was a simple thing of beauty, it almost worked like Mary Poppins' magical spoonful of sugar. I had seen it modeled by a former teacher of the year and it was one of those things that I kept in my teacher toolbox of techniques. I didn't realize that the "Catch a bubble!" technique was deliberately created to increase student compliance and has its roots in racial bias, where it was developed to keep students of color quiet. That technique, combined with other racially biased policies such as walking quietly and silently in a straight line, contributes to the school-to-prison pipeline. I felt like I had been punched in the gut as I began asking questions and considering current educational practices. I knew that something radically different had to take place. I knew at that moment that our structure and system of education in this nation had to change and look completely different than it had looked years prior. Our entire system is based on racist practices, and we wonder why things aren't getting better.

We can't play it safe anymore. The inequities must be confronted. This requires bold, brave change! It will require us to pioneer a new way of thinking about education. It is through this brave, new world that we will be able to give our children the education that honors who they are and prepares them for a world that needs them.

ABC'S: THE BUILDING
BLOCKS OF EDUCATION:
ATTENDANCE

*"Some know the value of education by having it. I
know its value by not having it."*
-Frederick Douglass

Over twenty years ago, a young Missouri boy made
local headlines when he went missing in a small rural
town just an hour outside of the St. Louis Metro area.
He was abducted while riding his lime green bicycle by a
man who was driving in the area, miles from his home.
For years, the boy's family prayed, worried, and held
onto hope that he would be found. Nearly fifteen years
ago, the same boy made national headlines when the
seemingly impossible happened and he was found alive.
A tip had come through because another young boy had
been abducted a week earlier and when police arrived to
investigate, they discovered another boy was in the
house. His name was Shawn Hornbeck. Shawn's family
had never given up, spending thousands of dollars to hire
investigators to assist the local police force to help find
him. It would soon be revealed that when Shawn was
abducted, he was taken to live in a bustling, metropolitan
suburb of St. Louis, spending the last several years in a
busy apartment complex, near the city hall. On one
occasion he was questioned by a local police officer who

noticed a school-aged boy riding his bicycle on what was considered to be an ordinary school day.

Shawn reportedly told the police officer when he was stopped and asked why he wasn't in school that he "was homeschooled." The police officer left, suspecting nothing out of the ordinary.

Before homeschooling was a known cultural phenomenon, the stares and conversations that would pop up were intimidating. Frequent grocery store conversations with our cashiers were perhaps the most dreaded because we were there for what felt like an eternity.

"How old are you?" A cashier once asked me. We came to know her as Candace. She had kind brown eyes and short brown hair. The burgundy work vest she had to wear complimented her olive complexion. I loved her pins on the lapel. They changed with the seasons, and they helped me feel connected to Mamo, who adored lapel pins from the Avon catalog. It was comforting to feel connected to someone outside of the house because often I would go a couple weeks without seeing any adult other than my parents.

My blue eyes met her own. I had already been coached on what I was supposed to say.

"I'm nine," I replied.

"What grade does that make you in?" She asked.

I shifted the weight of my feet, squirming. I actually had no idea. My mom sensed my nervousness. "Third grade," Mom answered for me, sparing us both embarrassment.

"Ah...shouldn't you be in school?" Candace asked, her tone concerned.

"I'm homeschooled," I quipped.

"Oh, that must be nice." This time her tone was more condescending. "Isn't that illegal?"

The following few minutes were a conversation where my mom explained the legality of homeschooling and reassured Candace that we were learning home economics while gathering cans of green beans to put in the cart and that we weren't just laying around in our pajamas all day. Except we were.

No one, with the exception of my grandma, noticed that we weren't progressing in our education. By the time I graduated high school, I hadn't completed anything in a sequential, scaffolded order. Math workbooks, where skills are built upon by taking things in a logical order were sporadically completed in a disorganized manner. One elementary book would take me two or three years to complete. High school workbooks were non-existent. My mom was busy building the movement, so it was easier for me to skip a day, learning how to be a little Susie homemaker, then to understand algebra.

While reading and writing came naturally to me, math and science did not. I would plead for my mom to pull herself away from the phone coaching other homeschool mothers so she could help me with upper-level math. I had no idea what I was learning or how to access the content. My mom and I would have sporadic sessions where she would attempt to tutor me on the concept of the day; be it algebra or geometry. Calculus, trigonometry, college algebra? They seemed as out of reach as me dating my celebrity crush (Number 19, Brendan Shanahan from the St. Louis Blues). These sessions would be short lived. I didn't have the foundation in math to understand the concept, she didn't have the patience or ability to teach it to me. Ending in frustration and tears, as I watched my dream of Ivy League school slip through my fingers with every defeating word problem, I would get angry and huff off to my room.

The sad part is that I would go days without completing any schoolwork, or at least, any school that was structured or traditional in a sense. Though our state had laws that regulated the number of hours of instruction we were supposed to get annually, there was no one to ensure that we were actually attending home school. Lesson plans and hours were not logged, though required through our homeschooling law to verify that regular, consistent education had taken place.

I had enough drive and IQ that I was able to make up for the deficit in my supposed education.

Divine Intervention. I had been blessed with the ability to construct meaning of things and grasp concepts at a crazy quick rate.

My brother was not as fortunate. His elementary education was severely neglected. Being the oldest, and loudest, I demanded more attention. I was not content to not learn and to go days without doing school. I was my own advocate. My brother though, a few years younger than myself, spent most of his early, formative years playing GI Joes and Playmobil on the floor of the living room. He was imaginative and inquisitive but struggled with academics. He struggled with reading. My mom brushed it off, citing homeschool advocate authors Raymond and Dorothy Moore's book, *Better Late than*

Early. This book discusses the benefits of waiting until your child is older than seven to begin formalized instruction. When my brother finally learned to read at nearly ten, my mom cited this as a success.

Except it wasn't.

The lack of oversight into whether homeschool children are getting regular, consistent education is a component that homeschool parents say preserves their freedoms and rights to do what is best for their children. They don't want the accountability that ensures that their children are attending school regularly. While there are parents who homeschool that do ensure their children are attending school regularly, there are just as many, if not more, parents who do not.

In 2017, a horrific case occurred in California. One incredibly brave young girl broke free from the prison of her home and placed a phone call with the aid of her older siblings to 911. She had never been outside before on the street. She asked for help rescuing her and her twelve brothers and sisters. She had been homeschooled her entire life along with her siblings. Jordan Turpin and her siblings were found in one of the most horrific cases of child abuse and neglect that law enforcement in California had ever discovered. Little ones chained to beds, sitting in filth, barely able to eat. Severely malnourished and educationally neglected, these children had not received credible homeschool education. The Turpin's parents were found and convicted of 25 years to life for the abuse that they did to their children. Social workers and anyone that could peek in on the validity of instruction these children were receiving under the guise of being homeschooled had been strangely absent.

When I had pneumonia at seventeen, it was highly probable that I could have died had not some form of divine and medical intervention occurred. The scary thing is that no one would have known. At least, no one would have known for a little while. Putting compulsory attendance measures in place would help to ensure that there are decreased numbers of homeschool students who are abused and neglected. This starts with the legislative process at local state levels and it's an uphill battle for those who, such as The Coalition for Responsible Homeschooling, have sought to draw awareness to and get started over recent years.

No doubt passing laws to ensure that homeschool students are attending school is a lofty goal, but we should not grow weary in doing good. Laws are needed in every state to ensure that students who are homeschooled have the right to receive an education that their public and private school peers do. Though that education may look different, requiring compulsory attendance for these students would help to ensure their right to an education is being honored and upheld. This should not come as a threat to parents who truly want the very best educational opportunities for their children. In addition, there is a need to increase the number of social service workers through increased funding.

When kids who attend public schools are absent for a predetermined number of days, the teacher, principal, counselors, and attendance committee know. Though it varies district to district on the number of days that are acceptable for a student to miss instruction, it is still a universal requirement that when students miss a certain number of days without any documentation then it is necessary to intervene on that child's behalf to ensure that they are being educated properly. Social workers are able to pay a visit to the home and determine if the child is safe or has needs that can be addressed. It's not because it's a "gotcha" idea, although hot lining the neglect or abuse is a part of the accountability measure here, it's because sometimes families struggle to provide for their children. Sometimes, transportation issues arise, and kids can't get to school. Sometimes, a crisis occurs. Sometimes a family needs help, and there should be no shame in that. In the words of the old African Proverb, "It takes a village to raise a child."

Schools understand that tracking attendance is vital to a child's well-being. The federal government values this component so much that they directly tie federal funds to attendance rates. Schools know, and teachers understand, that if a student misses more than a few days, that their education can suffer. We understand that it is important to the well-being of a community to help struggling families and students and to ensure that they are in school. We know that when students are failing in school the first thing to do is look at their attendance to determine any patterns. Are they late? Do they skip every Wednesday? We ask and answer the hard questions and apply the correct answers if we can. If I had been in school, my school would have soon learned that I was sick. This would have prompted the need for doctor's notes and absence excusals.

My parents could have potentially been set up with medical resources and if needed, I could have been set up with home-bound services. As it was, I was invisible. I could have as easily vanished, and no one would have known the difference.

What would you say if I told you that there are homeschool children I grew up with that now, at 30 and 40 years old and older, are living with their parents, who are required to give any money they earn to their parents? What if I told you these same adult children do not have a social security card or a birth certificate? What if I said these same adults do not have driver's licenses or access to social media or relationships with others whom they could potentially build a life with apart from their parents? This is a common reality. The Winters' oldest three children are still caught in this cult of control. Eliza broke free around the same time that I did and her parents disowned her. Their solution was to buckle down and move to the middle of rural Missouri, away from civilization and take their children with them, effectively keeping them hostage to this day. With no accountability, no record of school attendance, these children are lost in the system. No one knows they exist. They, like the 20-something-year-old Turpin siblings, are lost to a world who should be experiencing everything amazing their uniqueness offers. Instead, they are serving their parents, with their lights hiding under a bushel. We can't allow lax homeschool laws to manipulate adult and children's lives any longer.

Transparency and accountability are needed to ensure that homeschool students are receiving adequate education. We can't let insufficient laws foster environments that can be harbors of abuse and neglect. We can't snuff out their lights through our inaction.

ABC'S: THE BUILDING
BLOCKS OF EDUCATION:
BEHAVIOR

"No significant learning can occur without a
significant relationship."
-James Comer

I loved being assigned students on my classroom roster that had struggled to be successful in previous classrooms. These were students who were diamonds in the rough, as I liked to say. They needed patience, a teacher who was informed on mental health and trauma, and someone to still hold them to high expectations without triggering them. By the end of their time with me, as was generally the case, their behaviors would dissipate, and many times disappear altogether as they realized they were safe, and their brains began to heal from the trauma they were exposed to. I was the teacher who would be warned about student behavior. I would be warned about how a student that was in my classroom was prone to throwing objects, or maybe they had been known to hit, kick, or be physical in some way towards others. I tried not to listen to that. I believed every child deserved grace and forgiveness, wiping the slate clean each day, each month, each new school year by not allowing previous notes and files to influence my opinions.

I tried very hard not to ask or know about students before they had a chance to show me who they were. I always reiterated that to my Sparkling Scholars at the beginning of the year. They were amazed. In time, they came to understand that they were responsible for the story they would write about themselves and that they had a teacher who was not only a cheerleader, but someone who was a mentor and advocate, too.

I was a young teacher, who had not even graduated college, when I first watched Rita Pierson's TedTalk titled, *Every Child Deserves a Champion.* It gripped me and changed me forever. She was a black woman with a passion for education. I didn't get the opportunity to learn and grow from black educators, never in college or university, and she was a gem and the first mentor I had. Her TedTalk has since been viewed millions of times. She spoke on educational reform and had a big love for children and building relationships with your students. "Kids won't learn from someone they don't like," she said. It's true. And you can't fool kids either into thinking you like them, when deep down, you don't. Kids are smart and can sense inauthenticity.

I loved telling my Sparkling Scholars that the principal always placed the best students with the best teacher so that together, we could have the best class. It was amazing to see how these kids would look at each other, knowing that they likely weren't all "the best" students by their definitions and take hold of this phrase. They would latch on to it, like they were holding onto a lifeline. Together, we would build connections and powerful bonds that would carry us through whatever collective traumas and celebrations we may have found ourselves in.

It was exhausting though, to be "that teacher." I was the teacher who got the severe behaviors because I knew and understood childhood trauma and the power of student advocacy.

Every student in my room had a voice, they had choices in how to conduct their day, and they were empowered with the ability to be their own advocate for what they needed to be successful in their education. While exceedingly effective in my classroom management, it wore me out. I had to be two steps ahead of students all the time, thinking of all the possible scenarios and what-ifs. I wasn't alone in that feeling. There were strong, veteran teachers who would tell me frequently that they were tired and worn out. They voiced frustration of always being the teacher to be assigned the challenging students because it eventually took its toll. It was emotionally exhausting. This would make these veteran teachers consider retirement and simultaneously pray that for once in a long string of years, they could experience a break.

My more recent years of teaching revealed a more troubling trend in dealing with student behaviors. Students were being held to fewer and fewer standards, and often, discipline from administration was nothing more than a talking to. Very rarely was a consequence administered. It felt like administrators were afraid to discipline, for fear of possible parental retaliation or being accused of discrimination. While understandable, this has created classrooms and scenarios where we no longer expect students to adhere to expectations and where teachers and students don't feel safe in their own classroom.

Some of the stories that teachers have told to one another would make the most decent citizen wonder, "How did we get here?"

Very often new teachers with limited classroom experience must be willing to work in school districts that are less than ideal for a number of reasons when entering the profession for the first time. This often lands teachers in inner-city schools or rural schools where the pay is low, and commutes are tough. A young teacher once told me about a situation that occurred in her classroom, in an inner-city school district, when she was six months pregnant. A third grader showed up to her classroom with a BB gun. She had struggled to establish a connection with him, and her principal did little to facilitate her need for disciplinary support. He held all of his classmates and his teacher at gunpoint against a wall. He was given one week of out of school suspension. He came back to her classroom the following week.

Another teacher friend who is no longer in the classroom recounted to me the PTSD that she developed from students who threw keyboards at her, stabbed her hands and face with pencils, threw chairs at her, broke her arm, and tormented his classmates with similar escapades. We went to college together and were both passionate about teaching. Her passion and amazing contributions she would bring to a classroom vanished when she was asked to consistently endure this type of abuse, daily. She was one of those teachers that statistics say don't make it past year five. It had nothing to do with her ability and everything to do with her mental health.

My own boys for much of their lives went to a school district where character education took a backseat to academic performance. The schools were quite large, and students easily slipped through the cracks. My boys dealt with two active shooter situations while they attended there. Bullying was pervasive and it went unaddressed. Students were "talked to." They served minor lunch detentions. This leads to a poor school culture and a situation where kids and teachers didn't feel safe.

My oldest was a target of extensive bullying during his sixth, seventh, and eighth grade years. Every day in sixth grade, he was excluded from lunch. As soon as he would sit down, the entire table would get up and walk away from him. He was targeted due to his neuro-divergence and called, "gay" as a derogatory term. Despite meetings with multiple administrators, school resource officers, staff, and teachers, no consequences were handed out to the offenders. A year later, a friend of his he had gone to school with since kindergarten experienced the same level of bullying and harassment from girls in their school.

She had reportedly told the school counselor that she was seriously contemplating suicide. Though the school knew this, they sent her home without, allegedly, any intervention. She went home on the bus. When her little brother arrived home an hour later, he found his older sister dead, hanging from the ceiling fan in her room.

Teachers in classrooms across America are trained extensively for school shooter scenarios and intruder drills. We are told by our districts and schools that even if a social media platform, such as TikTok, serves as a means to facilitate a viral trend such as a "National School Shooting Day," that we are to report to work. Teachers experience behaviors from students yelling insults at them, writing threatening notes of hatred towards them, and throwing objects at them. When we ask for support, our students are barely spoken to either at home or by administration. Rarely will a student be made to miss out on a reward (such as a field trip, assembly, or other special occasion).

The students that consistently do the right thing and adhere to school expectations have for years voiced to me their frustration at not being recognized for doing what is expected. They have felt that those students who break the expectations and rules of school often get special treatment and partake in those things that others have worked hard for. It isn't just.

When I taught, I had a phrase that I would use in case we needed to clear the room for a student who decided to empty shelves, hurl objects, and tip over desks. My phrase was, "Ice cream!" and we would practice clearing out the room to be prepared. We practiced for intruder drills. Though students never knew what type of intruder we were practicing for, I did. All the teachers did. We generally prepared for angry parents or students. I say we "knew" but really, it was the proverbial elephant in the room. We may have whispered it to our teacher bestie next to us at professional development, but no one ever mentioned it to the entire room.

Yet, we all knew who would come through the doors or be on premises should this occur.

Teachers and students shouldn't be asked to work in a situation where we are preparing to lose our lives for hostile, violent parents, and former students. We are made to be trained in restraint holds in the event there is a student that wants to run away from the classroom or is violent towards someone. We are made to learn how to block students who bite and spit and learn how to get out of a hair-grab (every weave wearer's worst nightmare). We are essentially told that this is normative and that we need to do what we can to ensure the safety of the student who is engaged in physical aggression. It is twisted and has contributed to the gaslighting of teachers. We have been conditioned to believe that preparing for intruders and deescalating physical aggression is a normal part of our job. There is nothing normal about this! We have let aggressive behaviors go unchecked.

Parents throw caution to the wind and blindly take their child's side. In my experience teachers such as myself have recounted how parents now bully, harass, and intimidate them. Parents are convinced that education is somehow al la carte, and they want institutionalized education to be customized to fit their child. When they don't get their way, parents bite. Children, while their voices *are* valid, often go home and report to their parents their interpretation of what happened at school that day.

It is not always accurate. Teachers and parents are a team, working for the betterment of their common goal: the child. Children are good at knowing how to play one side against another to weasel out of consequences. This is a frequent occurrence between moms and dads, divorced households, or grandparents and parents. It is not different at school. Assuming goodwill on the part of parents and teachers would help to mend this riff that has grown into a deep divide.

Teachers show up to school every day (generally speaking, there are exceptions which is important to note) wanting to do the very best that they can for other people's children whom they very much love as if they were their own. Hearing that they are constantly missing the mark, not understanding, or providing enough compassion and interventions for behaviorally disordered and/or traumatized students, is like a knife into our teacher's heart and soul. We lose sleep over other people's children because they are our own.

Teachers can't continue to teach in these conditions. Indeed, we aren't. Students with trauma and extreme behaviors need support. They need to be supported by a team of professionals who aren't already overwhelmed with caseloads. This means we need more staff, which means more funding. We need for administrators to not listen to the random email that an entitled, angry, helicopter parent sent because a teacher gave their student an appropriate consequence. We need parents to support teachers. We need the parents who think they can do it better, to simply remove their child and look for educational alternatives. If they aren't in that position? They need to shut up, sit down, and take their granny panties out of a wad.

And while they are straightening their panties, they should take a moment and consider writing a letter of appreciation and support for their child's teacher. I can promise you that thank-you letters are better than any

PTO lunch or gift card ever purchased. Those thank-you notes are among the items that teachers never throw away because they know that they just may need to pull them out on a day when they've spilled tears over a student whose parents don't value what they are doing for their child.

And someday, those same letters and tokens of appreciation might be found by someone's granddaughter. That's how much of an imprint those make on the heart of a teacher.

ABC'S: THE BUILDING
BLOCKS OF EDUCATION:
COLLABORATION

She had short brown hair, was slender, and had a laugh that sounded like wisdom. We had both been hired together, to teach the same grade and content area. We were going to be the new third grade reading teachers. We were in my room sorting through books that had been left by the previous teachers. I was nervous. I had really strong ideas on the ways that young students needed to learn and access literacy and as is often the case with teachers who teach reading- you can have a lot of passionate, opinionated ideas on the best way to go about doing it. I wasn't sure what her take on reading instruction was going to be, but I knew that if we were both going to be successful that we would have to get one thing right. We were going to have to effectively collaborate.

Collaboration, or working together as a team with common goals and providing feedback on student success, was weak in every school I had taught in. Teachers would walk into a collaboration meeting with their principal and the collaboration would halt. There was something amiss, an air of mistrust and a lack of wanting to be vulnerable, all things that are needed to have effective collaboration. Collaboration is what drives student and school success and when it isn't going well or happening at all that is a concern.

It's a bit like asking a team of builders to build a home without a road map or specific instructions on what parts of the house they are building.

Are they working on the foundation? Plumbing? Detail work? Framing? If their plans are poorly laid out, or they don't discuss with one another when certain phases are done or how those phases impact one another, there are problems with the structure of the house.

Jane broke the thawing ice. "What do you think about book reports?"

My head popped up over the stack of books I was sorting through. My eyes widened. It was the perfect question to gauge how I approached teaching reading. I answered honestly.

"I hate them," I stated matter-of-factly. I winced quickly as I thought for a bit about the impact that opinion could have on our working relationship.

"Really? Do you really?" She said, eyes wide with anticipation. I nodded my head. "Me too," she said. "I was so afraid you were going to say you loved them," Jane giggled.

The next four hours was the beginning of our friendship. We talked about our vision for third grade, different theorists that we wanted to use, and research-based practices. We talked about our favorite books and how we wanted to go about facilitating a love of reading in our scholars.

She came from middle school and knew all the current middle school theorists and I came from the land of little people and knew about things she had never heard of like guided reading and phonics instruction. I knew the theorists she was unfamiliar with and together, we created a symbiotic relationship that centered heavily on collaboration.

Over the next two years, we grew, and our students grew with us. Students that came to us not comprehending third grade books, left our rooms at the end of the year having nearly made up their gaps and in many cases, surpassed them. Our building wide data was excellent for third grade, especially in year two once we had our systems in order. Student engagement, especially among reluctant readers, was high. We were both recognized as being leaders in literacy and we were asked to join the literacy leadership team. This team helped to write curriculum and provide vision for reading and writing instruction for all teachers and students that our district served. We eagerly discussed data daily, sharing scores and reflecting on struggling students that we both had. We shared strategies and new things we were learning on a daily basis. We gladly shared our tests and grades with one another, very often grading them together late into the night. We knew each other's kids and we knew where they stood in relation to achieving a learning objective. We were the dream team.

I had never been in a teaching role before, or since, that had collaboration like the one that Jane and I had. I have reflected on collaborative teams I have had, and that all teachers have had, and asked myself, "What made this one so great?" We truly were the model of what districts say they want when it comes to collaboration.

Teachers are pressured to collaborate with one another, to share student data and to analyze, and to plan instruction together. It doesn't usually work though.

What was far more typical in my experience was awkward, forced conversations around student data with our principal during weekly collaboration meetings. There was generally a pretty intense air of competition among teachers in high pressure districts from my experience. There was a lack of trust as well, where teachers felt that if they shared their struggling students' data with another colleague, they may be judged as not being effective. The fear was that information would get back to the principal and then your evaluation reflects ineffectiveness. The pressure to collaborate and share with your principal was about putting your own best foot forward. It wasn't true collaboration; it was like forcing a square peg into a round hole. This led to toxic team traits where there is a lack of trust, transparency, and togetherness. It was miserable and stressful, trying to make something that was broken work.

Collaboration, whether you are in the educational field or not, has become a buzzword in recent years. Collaboration and healthy teams are the driving force in all industries today. Sharing ideas, data, and analysis of goals is how businesses and corporations grow. It's an important skill to master because when collaboration goes well, it brings about greater job satisfaction and productivity. Everyone benefits when collaborative practices are strong. Educators have known this for a long time.

So, what made Jane and I's collaborative relationship work? What gave us this sense of trust, transparency, and togetherness that led to a healthy team? What lessons can be learned from this golden egg?

First, time leads to trust. We spent hours together, outside of school and before school started. Working in a district that allowed us to come and go in our classrooms whenever we wanted, allowed us flexibility to devote the time we needed to the tasks at hand. Before school started, we were allowed to come in and work for as many days as we needed, as many hours as we felt were necessary to work on either that which made our teacher hearts happy, or what was needed. We did things that were outside of school, like coffee dates and happy hours. We talked on the phone and texted. Those first few weeks of school when we were brand new to our district, no one once sent out an email demanding we spend time in our classrooms. Not a single administrator sent any emails or to-do lists ahead of the reported workday.

Throughout our time there, it was apparent that our district trusted us and granted us the gift of time. They trusted us to do our job and celebrated when anyone was recognized as doing something well. Teachers in this district had the energy to have Pinterest-worthy rooms if they chose. Teachers here were beyond coworkers, they were friends. The thing that we had in common throughout was that our district guarded our time. They recognized and stated from the top that having boundaries was acceptable. It was genuinely not expected to read work emails before contracted time.

It was completely acceptable for teachers to take a vacation in the middle of the year and go all summer without responding to emails. Your time off was honored. Administrators modeled this well, not being afraid to take off if needed during the school year or sharing about their vacations they took over Christmas break or summer vacation. Knowing that our time was honored, led to us being able to trust our leaders to do what was in our best interest.

Beyond that, professional development embedded strategic work time and often we were given workdays. Everything had a purpose and was intentional. When professional development was necessary, the goals were abundantly clear. Everything was connected to the actual work we were doing in the classroom. Our time wasn't wasted. Our plan time was our plan time, and we knew ahead of schedule when there were meetings that would ask us to give up our plan time. Time is a gift. Having a district that facilitated spending time together, that gave us time to work, and honored our boundaries and personal lives allowed Jane and I to have the time we needed to spend together to establish trust. We were able to foster a relationship together because we were given the gift of time, with no questions asked, and few expectations placed on it. Our schedules and pacing within our classrooms were not rushed and moving and break-neck speed. Projects that were important to teachers went untouched. Jane and I wanted to encourage our kids to read more independently, so we met with them weekly to discuss their independent reading goals. This led to a massive third grade slime party at the end of the school year, if they were able to read a predetermined number of independent books. Yes, my room was covered in slime, and I may have been crazy for doing it, but it was such a joy to allow my kids to look forward to accomplishing a goal. Jane and I loved to read books aloud to our students, and in order to do that, we had to have time. We were never asked to justify the time we spent on these things. We embedded standards and learning objectives into the book we would read aloud, and the learning was deep, all while building classroom community. When we finished a read aloud, we would add it to our list of books we would celebrate at the end of the year. We would incorporate food and customs that were discussed in each of our read alouds into a huge book celebration after our state testing. We would do March Madness and have the entire school vote on a book of the year, pairing various books together in brackets. Other teachers would spend time on an old-fashioned Christmas pageant, or time-honored traditions of celebrating grandparents and veterans. Again, none of this was questioned.

The point is, our district recognized that the time teachers chose to devote to things that were important to them brought a level of joy. It brought us closer together because we were not always striving to meet the next goal, the next learning target feeling worn out from always running to the next never-ending task. They recognized that learning should be fun and that it was ok to devote time to something you were passionate and crazy about.

Secondly, because trust was established through time, transparency was able to be reached. Relationship experts will tell you that while time helps create lasting bonds, it is trust that is essential to the success of any single relationship. Without trust, you can't have a healthy relationship and you can't have a healthy team or workplace. Often, teachers trust one another but when asked to collaborate in a structured setting with one of your administrators, trust becomes absent. Our district and principals trusted their teachers, and it was felt from the top. I never wondered when they came into my classroom if they were going to nit-pick my lesson to death or if they were going to be suspicious about what I was doing. They smiled upon entry, talked to me and my students, and provided positive feedback. I felt valued and I felt seen. These things helped me to feel I could trust my administrator so that when we were asked to collaborate, I didn't feel defensive or that I would have to justify my decisions in the classroom. This created space to be vulnerable. Teachers were vulnerable with each other and with our principal. We were transparent about struggling students and weren't made to feel judged or inadequate when we had students who weren't meeting the target.

Jane and I trusted one another, and we were able to be transparent with our data. If she had a struggling student who wasn't mastering a concept, she would bring their work to me to analyze and vise-versa. We would provide strategies to try and ask questions about what we had attempted to get that struggling reader to grow. It was the way collaboration was supposed to be. When our students took a benchmark assessment, rarely did the results surprise us. We knew where our students were still growing, and we knew the stories they carried with them when they walked through the door. We knew where their strengths lied and where they shined brightest. Our students also trusted us with their stories because we were able to give them time to talk to us and time to work. When we made a promise to our students that we would have a celebration of some kind, or that we would be able to work on something together, it happened. Having time to do what we promised helped to establish trust. When students trust their teacher, learning can happen because they feel safe.

Trust and transparency are critical to the health of any organization. Yet, it extends beyond the workplace and actual job duties. For Jane and me, we trusted each other with our personal lives too. If her little guy was sick or she had a rough morning and was running late, she would call me, and I would grab her students. For me, it was being transparent about how my marriage was falling apart and how stuck I had felt with my abusive ex-husband. This was important to share with her because it sometimes did impact my ability to be my best, or to think about school. She helped to carry the mental load when I was some days just struggling to show up to work and not cry.

Being transparent about what was happening, allowed us to have each other's backs. We were a true team, we won together, lost together, and lived life together.

Lastly, we had a spirit of togetherness. Our building was great at fostering relationships. Teachers were given permission to go out to lunch together, to host get-togethers and gatherings, and even to do the dreaded potlucks. We did fun things that brought us together. For Jane and me, it looked like raiding the candy out of my candy drawer or sorting through the candy at professional development. I always gave her my lemon starbursts; she gave me her strawberry. We brought coffee to each other, laughed over dirty jokes, and loved to share hilarious writing samples from our students. Every day, we were given a lunch break in the teacher's lunchroom. We were able to sit, eat lunch, and laugh. It brought us and our whole grade level team closer.

Infusing joy into our workday was something that we did well. We loved to laugh and were given permission to do so. We were given permission to have fun and be creative. We were given permission to cry and share what was hard in our lives (either in the classroom or in our personal lives). Indeed, this is why Principal Gerry Brooks is so popular amongst educators. He is hilarious, and brings people together through laughter, while sharing the truth.

One day, my principal called me into her office. I was known to work late into the night at school, sadly avoiding going home to my toxic homelife. For a while, I had been hearing these weird noises coming from the ceiling in my room. It was eerie, being in a school building that was over one hundred years old late at night, even in a safe, small town. I brushed it off as it was a building that was ancient, so it was prone to pops, cracks, and bangs.

I wasn't sure what she was getting at when she pulled up the security footage. I asked her what I was watching for.

"Just wait," she said coyly.

The footage kept rolling. I looked at the time stamp, it said 9:30pm. At first I thought that she was going to have me analyze one of my students but at this time stamp, I knew that couldn't be the case. I started to wonder what I was doing here because nothing was happening on the screen.

"Just keep looking," she said. And then, there it was.

"AHHH!!" I screamed as I jumped backwards, nearly peeing my pants from surprise. My principal laughed hysterically.

A racoon popped into the frame, falling from the ceiling tiles, and clinging onto the security camera. His little face peered hopelessly into the camera as he sharply fell. He quickly grabbed the electrical wires he had brought down with him and began swinging from the wires like a hairy, Midwestern version of a monkey swinging from a tree. And then, it got funnier.

Our night custodian, who had become my nighttime confidant and friend, went tearing through the hallways, hands over her head, arms flailing, and then scrambled into a nearby classroom, promptly slamming the door shut. Getting the racoon out of the building required several men, some maneuvering, and a late-night school raid. They discovered this little guy had been quite busy over my classroom, having placed several snacks from the kitchen in his home which happened to be right over my classroom. He must have been wanting to channel his inner Ulysses, the squirrel with the superpowers from the charming book we had recently read, titled *Flora and Ulysses*, by Kate DiCamillo. *Maybe he, too, wants to do something great. I wonder if he likes cheese puffs?* I smiled at the thought.

The next day, I placed a printout picture of a racoon on my principal's chair before the day started. The racoon became our unofficial school mascot. Taking the time to share in a good laugh, brought us together. My principal spent the entire day scaring the daylights out of her entire staff over a racoon that had created mischief in our school. She could have said she didn't have time and devoted her time to other tasks that needed her attention. But she didn't. She took the time to bring us together by infusing joy and humor into our day.

The lessons that can be learned about amazing collaborative practices aren't earth shattering. They are simple but far too easily understated and undervalued. In some ways we have over complicated things in our society. We think we can do things alone and forge our own way, living independent of one another, but we can't. Collaboration, when it is done correctly, benefits everyone within the system. It's an important takeaway for homeschoolers, who plan alone, and do things in isolation. Collaboration holds everyone accountable to ensure that students are successful and growing. This is where homeschooling falls short. Homeschoolers need to learn how to welcome accountability and collaboration so that their students are learning, growing, and getting what they need in their education. Refusing to be vulnerable, in any scenario, generally means you have something you want to hide or protect. I leave you with this quote from Brené Brown, whom I hope challenges you to push for healthy collaborative practices, no matter what sphere of influence you find yourself in.

"Vulnerability is not winning or losing; it's having the courage to show up and be seen when we have no control over the outcome. Vulnerability is not weakness; it's our greatest measure of courage."

Our world needs more of this right now.

THE POWER OF COMMUNITY

"Never doubt that a small group of thoughtful, committed citizens can change the world; indeed, it's the only thing that ever has."

-Margaret Mead

St. Louis has a long-standing tradition of priding ourselves on our educational excellence. We have left our mark on educational history, in the way that school buildings are now designed and built. Educational environments, especially in urban settings were transformed by the architect William Ittner who in the late 1800's was commissioned by St. Louis public schools to redesign their buildings. Ittner sought to transform the way that students in cities learn, by giving them beautiful, ornate buildings with attention to detail, landscaping, natural lighting, and cleanliness. In the nation, St. Louis sits comfortably in the top ten for the number of private schools per capita. We are home to a leading Ivy League school. As a result of this investment in educational outcomes, St. Louisan parents are deeply concerned about their child's welfare and schooling experience. They are generally committed to helping with volunteer opportunities in the classrooms and are themselves well-educated. We have had superintendents take failing urban schools and completely transform them into success stories, so much so, that these schools have made national news and headlines multiple times over in recent years.

And yet, our once prized urban city school model in St. Louis public schools that was hailed as being an example to emulate has fallen far from grace and continues to have a stigma associated with it.

The Delmar Divide in St. Louis accurately reflects Missouri's sordid history of segregation and racial divisions and in a microcosmic way, it reflects our nation. To the north side of Delmar, you have largely concentrated populations of low-income, African American families. To the south, largely concentrated populations of white, upper class, wealthy families. The Delmar Divide accurately depicts the segregation that is found within public schools in St. Louis. Within the boundaries of the Delmar Divide, on the north side are elementary schools with around a 95% rate of African American students. To the south, lie elementary schools with around a 73% rate of white students. The Delmar Divide stands in stark contrast, reverberating the disparity in resources among the north side and south side schools.

Resources for students, teachers, and schools, are known factors that help to raise achievement scores and improve overall educational quality. Having resources helps aid students in their access to educational programs such as art, music, sports programs, science, and engineering. Resources for learning help to ensure that students have the best reading and math curriculums. Critics have stated that resources don't correlate to excellent teaching, which I would agree with only in part. There are resources such as having the right number of social workers and counselors that absolutely have an impact on school culture, student learning and motivation, and the emotional well-being of everyone.

Resources help to make excellent teaching stronger, facilitating stronger opportunities for amazing teaching and learning to shine.

I was shocked when I learned that my own school district was facilitating the inequality of the distribution of resources. My friend Allison was an art teacher at one of our four elementary schools. She shared that our schools to the south of the Delmar Divide had an annual art budget of around $12,000 while the elementary schools to the north found themselves trying to foster a creative arts program of approximately $5000 annually. Schools in our district on the south side had the best PTO and were known to help provide additional financial resources to help with programs. Yet, on the north side, PTOs were a luxury. Our parents were working two and three jobs, often working overnight shifts. Forget the cute luncheons and gift bags, our families were trying to survive. When state testing rolled around, our schools on the north side struggled to find money in our budgets for student prizes to increase student motivation. Arguably, in our schools on the north side, increasing student motivation and engagement with the state benchmark test (which can take hours and is generally stretched over multiple days) should have been a priority as our scores were traditionally lower. Schools on the south side had higher scores and more money in their budgets for what makes learning fun, padded by their strong PTO and fundraising.

The disparity in the impact that resources have on learning can be seen in homeschooling as well. Resources in homeschooling are loudly downplayed by the majority who often try to negate the impact that learning resources can have on a child's educational quality and outcomes. This is often done to help validate a parent's inability to provide an adequate education for their children. Families who don't have the resources they need to homeschool well (either due to low income, high numbers of children, or both) are the loudest proponents of the "you don't need resources to homeschool" mantra. That was the experience I grew up in. "We don't need resources," I would hear my mom say. She would list the ways that homeschooling could be done for free to new homeschool moms. And indeed, that was my experience.

Much of my education was centered around going to the library and purchasing used curriculum at secondhand sales where outdated, previously used curriculum could be purchased for pennies on the dollar. Often, families who held to the idea that little investment was needed to ensure a solid educational outcome, were the same one's shopping exclusively at second-hand stores and ones who sought to homestead and live off the grid. Homeschool peers whose parents had far more financial means, were able to access things like college placement exams, college scholarships, and private tutors to set them up for success with tough subjects like high school calculus and physics. There was a clear advantage within homeschooling when students had adequate resources. These were the kids that went on to college.

One of the most powerful examples of how stakeholders and a community can positively impact the inequalities in education happened when I was teaching in Farmington. One of the parents of a student in my classroom, had a heart the size of Kenya and a love for others the size of its continent. Recognizing that many students in our school district were struggling to purchase school supplies due to poverty, she began a community wide campaign, enlisting the help of other parents who had more means within our school. Banding together, this small group of committed parents knocked on the door of every business in town. By the following school year, she had orchestrated having school supplies bought, purchased, and donated by local businesses for students. School supplies from that point forward were free of charge for every single student, kindergarten through twelfth grade from there on out. Her love of the school she grew up in and the love that the community had for students was transformative and nothing short of inspiring. I think that far too often, people underestimate their ability to have meaningful, impactful change when they are committed and passionate about a cause.

Resources are not just economic, though, they are also human. One of the success stories of the school in which I worked was the Reggio-Emilia model that was implemented at the Early Childhood Center where I subbed.

It was highly unusual for this model of education to be implemented within a public school and yet this principal, who had a strong vision and worked closely with our superintendent, rolled her dreams out and watched as her vision had a ripple effect. The district, prior to her arrival, was in danger of losing accreditation. Massive, transformative change was needed, and bold visionaries were a prerequisite to change the direction of this cruise liner. Implementing this model, where stakeholders are highly valued, parents are invited into the learning space and sought after to mentor young students, had a tremendous impact on the engagement and ownership that the community felt. Everyone was expected to play a role to help mold and model these young children, everyone had a vested interest in a successful outcome. The school reflected the needs of the community and teachers were regarded with the utmost respect. Teachers were guides and mentors, with every classroom taking on learning projects that spanned the length of a school year. Every classroom was unique, and every classroom had different projects they were working on, as the projects selected were based on the interests of the students. Every child had one hundred languages, and every classroom, a thousand. It was the teachers, parents, and community's responsibility to help unlock and translate them into learning that could be observed, guided, and directed. It was truly educational nirvana.

Centered around this school that acted as the glue was a community garden, where students grew plants, raised chickens, planted fruit trees, and then ate what they had grown for school lunches.

Parents were committed to helping ensure the success of the garden and it was the garden that bonded people together. Working with dirt, fostering compassion for living organisms, and taking care of the school helped people to feel connected to one another and to the community. The concept of community and connectedness began to take root, it flourished and grew all the way up to high school. The families that had been invested in their child's early formative years, took the model of connectedness to the elementary school, and beyond. I believe that it was through the power of engagement with the stakeholders and community that allowed this district to alter course to be the shining example that it is today.

And here we sit, two years post-covid where schools and all sense of community and connection have essentially been misplaced. I believe we are at a precipice where we will need to decide if community and connectedness will be worth it once more. Parents have lost their sense of trust, and yet want to trust schools. It's not easy to do that though when some parents have only just begun to see their child's classroom for the first time in two years. Our sense of connection has been lost and I wonder, will we find our way again? This loss of connection is what is fostering the mistrust that parents have for teachers and schools, the entitlement and pervasive selfishness that drives the angry parent to say rash, harmful, and damaging things.

This collective trauma of the worldwide pandemic that we have walked through has left its undeniable fingerprint in our lives. Teachers who are giving their lives, quite literally, to the educational outcomes of their students, because they love their students, have been met with selfish, entitled parents who respond in anger when something triggers them. Parents have learned how to bully teachers, writing emails to administration often accusing teachers of wrongdoing without thinking the best. They demand that masks be worn, or not worn, they want to censor teachers from talking about hard conversations regarding race. Teaching, by nature, is an act of unselfishness. You must give of yourself in some way in order to better enrich the lives of others. When this is met with blatant selfishness and mistrust on the parts of parents, this is where teachers wonder if this is worth the cost to their own emotional well-being.

Stakeholders in the community, grandparents, and volunteers, have taken an even harder hit. They don't have a reason to visit schools due to covid regulations, and I wonder, will they ever return? Will these essential volunteers we need emerge once again? Have they filled their time with other things and people? These are the volunteers that have carried our students who need a grandparent figure or have helped to maintain a school garden. These are the volunteers who have read to our kids and helped show them a multi-generational aspect of the love of reading.

Enter stage left, homeschooling in the covid world. Homeschooling became an established school norm during Covid.

Many people found themselves homeschooling when they didn't want to, others kept homeschooling after brick-and-mortar schools reopened. It was sloppy, the harried decisions that families were forced to make. With poor understanding of laws and what it takes to successfully homeschool, this has left homeschool students in jeopardy. Homeschooling during covid, was also a way for people who were experiencing high levels of anxiety regarding the pandemic to cope. Children who, during covid, were homeschooled often faced being at greater risk of abuse and harm. Fewer eyes and ears were removed, accountability was gone. With the absence of structural support, some of these haphazardly homeschooled children were shamefully victimized. There was no structure in place to hold their parents accountable.

At the root of the desire to homeschool under normal circumstances lies the seed of mistrust. There is some form of mistrust in order to propel a parent to make that decision, whether it be for religious or educational reasons, or a mixture of both. For homeschoolers who live on the extreme edge of worldviews, having a community generally means that everyone looks, acts, and thinks in the same ways. Communal living would be a component of what these homeschoolers would say is needed, to pull away from the world and insulate yourself with people who are exactly like yourself, looking for ways to live exclusively off the land, shutting everyone and everything else out.

In order to change what is broken in our educational system, and I believe our hurting, broken world, we need to foster a greater sense of community. Evil wins in darkness and flourishes in secrecy and isolation. We must forge our way together, joining forces to ensure that all students, regardless of educational backgrounds, have the opportunity for an appropriate, equal education.

This desire for connection and partnership, the need we have to rely on and trust one another through our vulnerability is what we will need to turn the toxic elements found in schooling systems today. The toxic elements of mistrust are causing the crumbling of our educational system and it will be through trust that it can be rebuilt. We need connection. We need a healthy community. It is the lack of community that I believe has caused the crumbling of St. Louis' public schools. Parents don't trust the system that has failed their children, for very good reason. There is a chasm, a disconnect and there is failure to understand the work that is happening in schools. It is going to take bravery, fortitude, and patience as we attempt to piece together what was imperfect before and is broken now.

The aftermath of World War II left the parents and small community in Reggio-Emilia Italy wanting more. The landscape of the world as they knew it had changed drastically from what they had once known. This community was deeply committed to ensuring that their children had collaboration and critical thinking skills which would help them with new ways to learn. They wanted to ensure that their children were taught to be open minded, tolerant, and kind.

Together, they worked to build a brighter, better future. Several members of the community, mostly women, worked together to build the type of school they wanted, investing in their future by selling horses, an old German army tank, and trucks left behind from the ravages of the war. Through their commitment to building an inspired future where their young people were able to achieve great things, an entire generation was changed. A few years later, educational theorist Loris Malaguzzi would popularize and solidify the Reggio-Emilia approach. An approach to learning that is so transformative, that it has changed every community it has touched since.

Jesus called us to go and make disciples. He called us to go and touch the world, showing kindness and light and love to a broken, hurting world. Being agents of peace in a world where peace is something people seek for as though it were an illusion, has the ability to be a breath of fresh Bel-Air. Jesus doesn't want us to underestimate the difference we can have on the world when we work together for good.

THIS LITTLE LIGHT OF MINE

"Let your light shine so brightly that others can see their way out of the dark."
-Katrina Mayer

"This little light of mine, I'm gonna let it shine! This little light of mine, I'm gonna let it shine!" This was one of my favorite songs I recall my mom singing to me, before my world went dark, and we moved from Fairfax. I was enchanted by her and this song. I loved how she would do the bushel with her hands, covering up the light. "Don't let Satan blow it out!" I would tuck that song in my head, belting it from my lungs, and go take my kittens to church.

My parents for all their flaws did get something right. They blessed me with my name. It was one of the more beautiful aspects of my life growing up, knowing the meaning of my name. It became my mantra when times got scary, and I found myself shrouded in an invisibility cloak of darkness.

Chandra Dyan. Moon Goddess. You outshine the stars in the heavens. I would replay this in my head like a broken, scratched record, hearing the voice of my mother leaving me with a whisper of a blessing, when she was incapable of giving me more.

I woke up one day, three years into my teaching career and I didn't even recognize the girl in the mirror. I was a shell of my former self.

The bubbly, creative, energetic, effervescent, stylish girl had become depressed, anxious, fearful, overweight, and beatdown. My light, my spark, my spirit had dimmed.

The jushe that made me, me, was gone from the light in my blue-green eyes. I knew I had to fight to find her. He had broken me, made me forget all that I was until I was literally a shell of my former self that I no longer recognized. My upbringing in purity culture had left me open to this soul crushing, light diminishing wounding. I had nothing left to give to anyone. I hated that I had let myself become a fractured version of myself. It terrified me to let my boys see their mom this way. I had to fight to restore what the locusts had eaten. In order to do that, I had to do what feels antithetical to the heart of every healer, mender, giver, mother, teacher: I had to put myself first. I had to dig deep into the wellsprings of my heart to pour into myself the self-love that I needed. I scheduled a therapist appointment the next day.

I sat on the robin's egg blue sofa of my new therapist's office. The next hour was brutal. She had me define a safe place, a physical location that I identified as feeling safe. *Mamo and Granddad's farm, just beyond the shed down by the old, rusty red water pump.* It was always sunny there it seemed, and it was here, just under the clothesline that I could eat strawberries, smell irises, and find pot-bellied kittens basking in the sun. Bretina, the cocker spaniel, would eat the giant grasshoppers out here, making me giggle.

This was a space no one else came to, it was just mine. The smell of cow manure, fresh dirt, hay, sunbaked kittens, and grass would waft into my nostrils. This was home.

Katherine walked me through reconnecting with my inner child and had me meet her there in this safe space where only Jesus and I existed. She had me mourn her losses and make promises to help give her what she needed. She had me give the little girl who desperately wanted love, the love that I was now capable of giving her. I wept. I promised to give her the love she deserved, to be the heroine she needed, the advocate she wanted, and the grace to forgive. I promised to help her rediscover herself and help her find her worth.

The next year was a whirlwind. If I hadn't had the teammate I had while I was going through this personal journey of self-love, I wouldn't have been an effective teacher that year. Our time and resources are finite and limited and giving all of my spare time to heal and love myself once again were taking their mental toll on me. I wasn't able to plan the way I wanted or needed to because the free time I had was spent working feverishly on counseling homework and reading about how to recover from codependency. Having an amazing teammate in Jane made this possible because teaching and having a personal crisis without a supportive, trauma-informed school are incompatible.

I began to change from the inside out. The light came back in my eyes. My hair even became healthier. I began to lose weight and found empowerment in making decisions for myself. My spark returned and I became stronger, as I fell in love with the woman that I had been created to be.

I shopped for clothes, did my nails, and got my hair done. I became unstoppable and the feelings of giving myself the love that I longed for and only had ever imperfectly had was euphoric.

That journey of self-love was pivotal and taught me so much about not settling for less than what I deserved. It was that journey that helped me to spot toxic and abusive relationships that were not healthy for me. It taught me that boundaries don't have to be understood by others to be valid for our hearts. Through being empowered, I realized something else.

Teaching today has become an abusive partnership.

The burgeoning weight of the world sometimes feels as if it rests on our shoulders as teachers. It's a heavy burden to bear, but we are here for it. We aren't consulted about the changes we see that need to happen in the systems of education, the changes that would directly impact our day-in and day-out work lives. Instead, lawmakers, lobbyists, parents, and business leaders generally decide what is best for schools. We allow others who have no training or real understanding of what it means to be effective in the classroom, tell us how to do our jobs and we willingly go along with an often-failed plan. We show up ready to do the hard and heavy and damn near impossible. We willingly trade our peace and inner sanctum in the name of helping others.

We minimize the verbal abuse from students and parents, explaining it away with excuses like, "That student has a lot of traumas going on at home," or, "That parent just needs to feel listened to."

We accept the tiny stabs to our hearts when we are told in evaluations that we aren't enough, that our performance isn't adequate, that we are failing our students, that though we try as hard as we can, we will never, ever, meet our administrator's approval. Every conference room and principal's office have a box of tissues. Why? Because we willingly subject ourselves to being berated, disrespected, devalued, and unheard by a broken system. We are mistreated, we feel strong things and we cry, we promise we will do better and try harder next time. We fix our mascara and help straighten each other's crowns. We dust the chalk dust off our Chicwish skirts, straighten our Peter Pan collars, and tell ourselves we will just have to research more, plan more engaging lessons, and work longer hours. We think if we do one more thing, reach one more unreachable student that somehow we will be loved and valued. We tell ourselves that this *Handmaid's Tale* we have found ourselves employed in is making an impact and a difference. *I am a changemaker, difference realizer, impact wave maker,* we whisper to ourselves in moments of doubt. And we are.

But if this were your best friend, and you knew they were caught in a domestically abusive partnership, you'd tell them to high tail it out of there. To place peace over security, safety over status quo.

Yet teachers stay in this same type of relationship only to realize after we have taught for longer than ten years, that the only real difference that teaching is having is on us. It has wreaked havoc in our lives as our kids have grown up waiting on mom to get their grading done so quality time can be spent together. We do grades at our kids sporting events, we lesson plan in doctor's waiting rooms.

We doubt ourselves and our worth the longer we are in the field, becoming jaded and cynical. We question the validity of our difference making abilities. We don't have time for things that make our own hearts sing, unless what makes our hearts sing is our career. We print off cute things we've laminated and cut them out, telling ourselves that cutting out slips of paper while watching the latest episode of *Abbott Elementary* is a hobby. We have lost our way. We don't recognize who we are outside of being a teacher. "I do it for the kids," has robbed us of our identity.

From the early colonial era to the late 1800's, men held the predominant role as teachers. Far from formalized in its profession this was generally done as a pastime of sorts on the part of the men, when the demands of our agrarian society were not as great such as planting and harvest cycles. In the late 1800's, when the landscape of the world changed and it became more industrialized, and men were needed in other fields, women were then welcomed into teaching.

When society, not long after, realized the value that structured education could have on children, and society, they sought to bring in as many women as possible to fill roles. Instead of women being heralded and revered for their contribution to education, they were subjugated to men who held the hiring roles and positions on boards. This helped to cement a largely patriarchal profession where women were placed in subservient positions while men held all the power.

Though the scale is slowly tipping, and women are breaking glass ceilings now more than ever, the antiquated gender norms within schools remain. Men predominantly hold the visionary and authoritarian roles in schools as principals and superintendents and maintain the power to hire, fire, and retain staff. Women largely remain classroom teachers and instructional coaches, holding lesser positions of power. Men in our schools write the evaluation systems and are on school boards, they are the theorists and the ones writing educational policy. Women historically have been in subservient, submissive roles finding their power and equality deferred to the men who created the systems they worked in.

It can take a long time for a partner in a toxic and abusive relationship to realize that the relationship was toxic from the beginning. The relationship isn't always toxic and abusive, or the abuser would have never been able to convince their partner to engage in a relationship with them. Viciously, the cycle begins where the empath doesn't please the abuser and has fallen from grace in the abuser's eyes. After a cycle of abusive behavior where the empath is gaslit into believing they were the problem, the empath accepts blame that was never theirs to own.

They promise to do better, to change, to be different in the hopes of gaining the affection and adoration the abuser once gave them. The abuser claims they were too harsh and gives gifts and notes of encouragement but nothing systemic ever changes in the relationship. This cycle repeats hundreds, if not thousands of times until the cloud lifts for the empath and they realize that they can't continue to subject themselves to the abusiveness and toxic traits. Or they stay.

Freeing oneself from the cloud of the abuser generally happens when the empath realizes one day that they no longer recognize who they are and that by adapting to the whim of the chronically unsatisfied abuser, they have completely lost their own personhood, integrity, and autonomy. They know that somehow they must get free. There are empaths who remain in these tragic relationships for years to come, sometimes staying at the expense of their own lives. They feel trapped and they don't see a way out. Others, take a bold risk and throw caution to the wind, desiring the fresh air of freedom sans security.

Over the course of time working in the schools has become a system that serves those who have money and power. Schools serve parents, business leaders, school board members, and administrators. Teachers are told we are too much or not enough and in either case, we promise to adapt and be flexible, changing our standards and personality to meet a subjective mark on an evaluation.

We willingly sacrifice taking care of our bodies, being able to eat when we are hungry and using the bathroom when we need to for the sake of being a better teacher. We promise to work under the threat of veiled verbal and emotional harassment and abuse, for the sake of our students. We allow others to dictate what we wear and when we wear it (Jean Day every Wednesday! Get ready!). We have subconsciously allowed education to become a toxic relationship that has become abusive. It's time to break free. We owe it to ourselves and to our own families to be the best version of ourselves. The world needs our voices, our unique talents, gifts, and passions. We are irreplaceable!

The single most compelling thing an abuser has to convince an empath to stay is the manipulation of their altruistic nature. We are told that the kids need us, and we fear what might happen to them if we leave. We bear the guilt of leaving solely on our shoulders when we know that to stay would mean a miserable, unbearable life. We tell ourselves that we can do it, for the sake of the kids. And slowly, the light has dimmed.

I used to tell myself that, too. I said I would stay in my abusive marriage for the sake of my boys. When I started to love myself, I realized that to stay in that relationship was causing my boys more harm than good. They needed to see a mom who had self-respect and who valued her own worth, not because of any performance factor but simply, because my mere life had value. They needed to see a healthy mom and a mom who could truly be there for them, a mom who valued her own life and modeled to them what it means to be completely healthy, from the inside out.

This is where yet another bizarre twist of intersectional fate comes into play. Homeschooling is rife with patriarchy; indeed, it is the only way that it has survived as long as it has. Women stay at home, submit to the men who earn the money and have the power in the relationship. Moms teach, dads work and oversee. This system is set up with a clear power differential. Children grow up witnessing dad having all the power, being able to leave the house in stylish business attire.

Dad comes home to tell his wife that her schooling, cooking, housekeeping, or child discipline doesn't measure up. Homeschooling would benefit from an upheaval of patriarchal values and systems. So would public and parochial schools. Many girls trapped in this system grow up not daring to dream beyond basket weaving skills and homemaking fantasies. Many boys grow up believing they don't have to do anything to earn respect, other than exist, no matter how awfully they may treat others.

I grew up watching the women in the religious right of the homeschooling world downplay the need for them to have an identity apart from child-rearing and homemaking. I watched through the years as my mom lost her sense of style, minimizing the need to exercise, take pride in your appearance, and spend the money needed to do so. I watched women wear the same clothes, year after year at homeschool conventions. Year after year, they appeared more tired, with another child on the way, and more depressed and lonelier.

Downplaying and minimizing the need for women to care about the way they look comes from this idea in I Peter 3:3-4:

"Do not let your adorning be external—the braiding of hair and the putting on of gold jewelry, or the clothing you wear— but let your adorning be the hidden person of the heart with the imperishable beauty of a gentle and quiet spirit, which in God's sight is very precious." (ESV)

I was told growing up that wearing makeup was a sin and that to care about your outward appearance was worldly. I grew up not knowing how to love myself because of the way this verse was used against me as I was growing as a young woman, learning how to express myself and my own individual style. This failure to help young girls think positively about their bodies, apart from biological purposes, sets girls up for finding themselves in abusive marriages and workplaces. It was spiritual abuse and it allowed domestic violence to reign, as all the patriarchal men had to do was remind the women to be quiet and gentle, hushing their autonomy, opinions, and personhood into submission. Patriarchy is bad for all of us, and it impacts our schooling structures negatively.

I left education when I realized that I was beginning to lose myself again after fighting so hard to find her. I was being censored by loud, racist voices in a wealthy community. I was told the books *Esperanza Rising,* by Pam Munoz Ryan, and *Refugee,* by Alan Gratz, were too controversial to be used. I had parents who wanted me to edit my personal Snapchat Bitmoji that I used in digital classroom components because I chose to wear the Black Lives Matter t-shirt on a cartoon graphic. I was told I was too much and not enough.

Students were allowed to bully teachers on group chats and write notes on everything that was said in class, with no consequences. My co-teacher and I were accused of lying. If I promised to do more, be more, and try harder I might meet their approval. I showed up to work with butterflies in my stomach daily, just like the cookies I would toss right before my ex-husband would fly into the driveway, waiting to verbally berate and abuse me. I left in tears every day. The feelings were all too familiar. I couldn't lose my light again.

Satan was trying hard to blow it out, to keep me small and keep my voice silenced. I left. There ain't no one gonna keep this light from shining. The world needed me to remember my jushe, my light and to fight to keep it. The world needs you, too.

THE GREAT RESIGNATION

"Systems don't change easily. Systems try to maintain themselves and seek equilibrium. To change a system, you need to shake it up, disrupt the equilibrium. That often requires conflict."

-Starhawk

Throughout history, every great revolutionary change has begun with an awareness that things are far worse than people have realized or cared to believe. They shake things up, go to war, abandon causes and fight for new ones. Harbingers have rung the bells from the towers for years, citing the impending doom of the collapse of American educational systems as we know it. Facebook groups, focus groups, and journalists across America reflect the groaning that teachers have felt for years, that has now reached critical levels.

It's no secret the issues that teachers have squarely faced in the last three decades. Parents have generally been problematic, so much so that when I was in college, I wrote an entire parent management plan alongside my classroom management plan that had administrators wanting to know more. Society has attacked teachers and our professionalism, degrading, and disrespecting our position, intelligence, and questioning our love for students.

Granted, these devaluations and generalized disrespect for teachers has not been without due cause. Teachers are broken, human people.

They are capable, just like police officers, doctors, and others, of doing heinous crimes to innocent children. Teachers are the first to hold one another accountable when a rotten apple has been discovered.

We are generally in this because we love to help, we have a gift for teaching content we are passionate about, and we have a fierce love for our students.

But somehow, this pandemic has created conditions that have accelerated this slow cooker educational crisis into more of an Instapot scenario. People have grown in their inability to communicate with any sort of grace and kindness. They attack teachers on social media using our names, locations, and schools. Parents appear at school board meetings and sue districts for attempting to keep their teachers safe and healthy. They have forgotten the power of words, neglecting even the smallest one-line email to let teachers know they are appreciated.

We are facing a grim reality. The federal and state governments have returned to their business-as-usual approach to enforcing accountability on school districts, pretending as if teachers can somehow magically make up the deficit in learning expectations from the last few years. Their expectations for how they will dole out money to districts have returned to pre-Covid normalcy, while teachers know that nothing will ever be the way it once was. Student benchmark assessments, data collection, teacher evaluations, all of it has returned as if Covid never happened.

But we know it did, and there isn't a single human soul who walks through the doors of any school who does not bear the weight of the scars of this worldwide pandemic.

We are not capable of supernatural miracles. We cannot erase what has happened to us. We are asked to participate in re-enactments at the beginning of the year, before students ever arrive, where law enforcement come in and pretend to be an intruder. We are given scores on if our brains were able to keep our students safe under this simulated trauma. Teachers can opt out if they have PTSD or health issues, as the simulation can be physical and triggering. We hate this professional development day, and we are expected to complete this training and then go set up our classrooms like nothing ever happened. No other space in the world prepares for massacres and intruders like schools do. Something is wrong that we have accepted that this is status quo within our schools today.

Students in urban areas will suffer the greatest when the inevitable collapse occurs, and more teachers begin to leave the profession. Teachers have felt the added pressure of teaching in urban schools for decades, due to the complexity of the issues that students and these schools face. Already at higher risk due to socio-economic statuses, students in urban settings will experience the injustice of not having a school bus that can get them to school because the school can't find enough bus drivers to run routes. Students in these areas will find their schools closing or being combined into other classes or absorbed into other buildings, creating overcrowding, and diminishing the quality of instruction they can receive. The systemic injustice and inequality in educational opportunities that are already pervasive will become insurmountable without drastic, swift, transformative change.

Teachers across America are leaving. We are underpaid and thought of as glorified babysitters. Indeed, we often feel that babysitting is what we do. When student behavior isn't addressed, sometimes just managing behavior becomes all you can do to get through the day. It takes a tremendous amount of skill, energy, and passion for a teacher to be able to manage behavior and teach. It absolutely can be done, but it leaves you feeling completely and utterly depleted at the end of the day. So, you begin to question your work-life balance because you don't have any.

Exhausted from being on your feet all day and pushing through the seemingly endless piles of administrative tasks has left you d-o-h-n done.

And you wonder, can you really do this for the rest of your life for what amounts to $16 an hour in an average teaching market? Teachers don't just have the summers off. We spend the first four weeks of summer in physical recovery mode, have three weeks that are purely ours, and the rest of the summer is spent in professional development, writing curriculum, and setting up our classroom. We start to wonder if I did something else what would it be?

As teachers have begun to leave, and college campuses are closing their teaching programs due to the lack of interest of new candidates, officials will have to make decisions about what the qualifications are to be a teacher. Considerations will have to be made about whether to do more virtual learning, where teachers can handle larger class sizes, or increased class sizes in already small classrooms. Parents will have to make decisions about what is best for their child, and it won't be a whole lot better in private school. Some students wouldn't be able to be accepted into a private school based on grades or income.

Homeschooling will become an answer that many will seek out. Many parents will need to continue to work, and kids will be at home, alone, teaching themselves. Laws for homeschooling are sloppy, lacking in any oversight or accountability. While homeschooling may be the answer for some, and can be a wonderful opportunity when done correctly, the need remains to ensure that these students are receiving an adequate education.

However, even the states with accountability have individuals who look over curriculum and lesson plans with little training. They lack the careful eye to know how to catch educational neglect. Many homeschool students in these states fall through the cracks, faring little better than students in states who don't. The lack of oversight helps to hide the shadows and evils of abuse and neglect and the harm that adults can do to children whom adults don't consider having rights.

It's a critical issue. Our children and our future generations depend on us to consider what education will be like when the teachers leave, class sizes are unmanageable, and a plethora of students are thrown into homeschooling. And I believe that teachers should leave. We have tried to make a broken, patriarchal, abusive structure work for too long and no one has listened. We have unnecessarily taken on more than we should, while continuously being underpaid and uncompensated. Our exodus will be the impetus that will cause the structure to experience a reformation. Mark my words, our educational system will collapse. The question is will we be ready for it. It will be an opportunity for others to envision what education would look like if we truly committed to addressing the educational inequalities within educational systems today. Together, we must rebuild from the ground up a stronger educational system that serves all students and teachers. This new system will need to look completely different than it has in the past.

Where does this leave us? What will the future of education look like? What will happen to the invisible children who are stuck in educational systems that lack the resources and support they require?

What will happen to the growing number of homeschooled students who will be educating and raising themselves because their parents still need to work due to the conditions of our economy, but don't want their children to be in a class of thirty or more students? What will happen to our communities as more and more schools close, and we lose touch with one another and our neighborhoods? Do we care at all?

THE CALL FOR SYSTEMIC TRANSFORMATION

"Ending educational inequality is going to require systemic change and long-term, sustained effort. There are no shortcuts and no magic bullets."
-Wendy Kopp

Fifty years ago, St. Louis began the country's largest desegregation attempt through our busing program as a result of a lawsuit from a group of concerned black parents in St. Louis city public schools who argued that the schools in St. Louis metropolitan area were not desegregated and providing equality in educational opportunities for their children when compared to the surrounding white suburbs. The outcome of the lawsuit was a transformative attempt to give students in St. Louis public schools the opportunity to access educational resources that were more plentiful in the suburbs through busing, seeking to address the transportation issues that the students in St. Louis faced. The hope was to increase diversity in white schools through the voluntary transfer of Black students to white suburban schools, while encouraging white students to attend city magnet schools, created as an outcome of the lawsuit. The goal was that by the end of the program, there would be 25% of Black students that would attend the St. Louis county schools. It was a massive, sweeping change, bold, and risky.

Though there have been individual success stories, today, the busing program boasts fewer black students participating, due in part to the end of funding for the desegregation program.

Some districts have seen an increase in diversity that has naturally happened, and they have dropped out of the voluntary program. Though it was a bold program that facilitated the creation of more magnet schools and helped to improve the quality of education that some students in the city received, it was not perfect. The lawsuit also wanted more resources to go to improve neighborhood city schools, which that improvement has not occurred. While the program positively impacted some students' lives, it was not nearly enough. Families did not always want their students to travel to attend school in a neighborhood that was not accepting of minority students due to the pervasively white population in the suburbs. Fifty years after the busing program was first conceptualized, there are fewer black students bussed into our white suburban counties today. Today, only two of the original sixteen St. Louis county school districts have higher rates of racial diversity. Today, the white and black segregation in our metropolitan area remains.

It was worth a try, this program. It was a brave, risky on taking hoping that this program would help to eliminate some of the racial segregation that has marked the topography of our riverside landscape. Nothing like this had been done before and we remain the largest busing program in the United States. Brave, risky, uncharted territorial change is what will be needed in order to provoke what is needed to improve our schools.

It requires the sweeping, swift change that has been brought on by brave superintendents and visionary principals that have turned non-accredited districts into nationally recognized ones.

Transformational, systemic change won't happen from pulling a measuring tape out of our magic satchel that reads, "Practically perfect in every way." It won't happen from a pinch of pixie dust or shouting, "Bibbidi-bobbidi-boo!" It will only happen from tireless work, enduring effort, and passionate investment from those that recognize if we don't pay the price now, our children will later.

Systemic change within education and its systems and structures won't be easy and it will require a sacrifice from every single person. We cannot think that we will improve the lives of the next generation by addressing the systems and structures that both overtly and covertly oppress women and children. We are all connected in some way. The lives of children, and the education they deserve, will not improve until the professional lives of those who care for them also improve. You cannot treat the symptoms; you have to holistically treat the source.

For years, teachers have been chronically underpaid when compared with other professions who have similarly educated and seasoned workers. Schools need teachers who know how to teach and can continue to reach the complex learning issues that impact young people today; issues such as learning and mental health disorders, intricacies of social media, and brain development. We need to prepare young people for a world with an uncertain future. This requires expertise. Expertise that requires compensation.

Leaving the profession has been made easier by the demoralization we have felt from being chronically underpaid, lack of support, and no hope in sight of raising society's level of respect for us. The stagnating wages are a hard sell in today's tough economy to encourage new teacher candidates. Fixing this will require buy-in from everyone, recognizing that teachers must be compensated adequately for what we do and the level of training and education we have. Teachers will vanish in droves and leave behind a massive hole that will need to be filled. These vacancies are already being filled with National Guards, untrained substitutes, and people who have degrees from unrelated fields. Teachers aren't just leaving because of parents, administration, overbearing secretarial tasks, or student behaviors. They are also leaving because of the pay. We simply can't make the math add up. Many of us in the nation are barely making enough and find ourselves just under the poverty line. We have realized we have more control over our salary if we decide to work elsewhere. In teaching, you don't have that ability, there is no negotiating, no bargaining, no opportunities for advancement without more student loan debt. In many states, teachers qualify for food stamps. In the traditionally corporate man's world negotiating for salaries, the ability to advance without significant debt accrued, and bargaining for benefits are common practices. Until we address the oppression that both the public and homeschool sectors have subjected women to, the children within those systems will continue to suffer.

Addressing the demoralization of educators and the systemic transformation that is needed should encompass a conversation on humanizing the profession. For years, teachers have stated how they feel that students have been reduced to being a number in an excel spreadsheet or statistic in aggregated data. Teachers have voiced their concerns that students are no longer viewed with dignity and humanity, but rather, as a data input field. I would propose that this shift in how student performance is widely viewed has also lent itself to viewing teachers as little more than data drivers and statistical analysts. They are the machine behind the numbers, and we are treated as such.

What is the purpose of education? That is the question we should be asking because within it lies the guideposts to fixing the problem that we seek a solution to. Education's goal is to create and foster intelligent, compassionate citizens who use their creativity and gifts to leave their imprint on the world, making it a better place than when they found it. This requires an altruistic nature on the part of any educator: education is meant for another individual, it is not meant to serve the educator's own personal gain or opinions. If education is to help facilitate kind, caring, intelligent citizens then how is it compassionate to not pay teachers what they are worth? To foster respect for them and what they do? How is it caring to suggest that human beings can live without basic needs being taken care of during a workday? How is it compassionate to leave behaviors within schools unaddressed for the students and teachers who wonder where justice is?

How is it kind and compassionate to allow educational neglect to happen to children who are invisible and forgotten? How is it humane to not immediately address the issues of inequality and systemic injustice to students of color?

Inequity in education is a universal issue that affects all of us because we are all connected. It impacts low-income students, minority students, students that are homeschooled, students who don't have advocacy or access to services that ensure they are getting an education free from neglect and abuse. It impacts the adults who work with them. It is up to us to ensure that the rightful education that belongs to every boy and girl in America gives them the opportunities they deserve to succeed in a world whose future is still being written.

It requires us to bridge the gaps between that which we don't understand and sometimes value. It requires us to hold ourselves to higher standards of altruism, greater regard for humanity and the feelings of others, kindness, respect, and empathy. These values aren't new, but they certainly feel forgotten in today's society. Nothing ruins our society faster than selfishness and self-centered ideals. Our children deserve better. Our future depends upon it.

It's time to get to work.

EPILOGUE: "THE END."

I closed the book, feeling a pang of bittersweetness, looking at the faces of my students looking back at me. Tears were shed on this journey, in the reading of *The One and Only Ivan*, a novel that taught us empathy, perseverance, loyalty, and the power of friendship. Daily, they could not wait for the mini lesson, because immediately following, was our read aloud time, embedded within our reading workshop. Daily, my Sparkling Scholars would gather on the carpet, around tables, desks, and wobbly stools. They would pull out their pillows and wrap arms around one another, holding on to every word as I read the story of Ivan, Stella, Bob, and Julia. Every year, when I introduced the book, their initial responses were as predictable as the circadian rhythms that hold our world together.

"Really, Ms. Hawkins? A book about *gorillas*?"

"That sounds so boring."

"Wait, there's an elephant?! What?"

"I don't know how I feel about this book. I'm not going to like it."

And every year, with every reading it was the most reluctant that ultimately became the most engaged with this tender, *Charlotte's Web*-esque book.

We cried when there was heartache, cheered and hooray-ed when justice was served, and marveled at the perseverance and devotion of a faithful friend's promise. And we learned. When the lessons were learned with the books we read together, and the last lines read, there was a holy pause as what we experienced sank in. The growth, the lessons, the joy, and the sorrow.

Applause. It was the appropriate response to every book we completed, always spontaneous and never elicited. Applause, followed by sadness as we realized that our beloved friends we were introduced to, were shelved for another class, another year.

Like anything that we open our hearts to, life teaches us about ourselves and our relationships with others. Our experiences open our eyes and show us who we are and what we are capable of. Our journeys can hold much wisdom for us when we open our hearts to the potential of being taught.

Like any good book, that challenges and shapes us, our lives can do the same. That was my experience with my own journey throughout life and education. It's not for the faint of heart, to take an honest look at oneself and realize that the fingerprints of trauma that linger on your life impact you in the present. It's not for the weak minded to recognize that your childhood was spent in shaping you to fear and mistrust others, and that you were raised with the ancient lies of racism and prejudice.

It takes a special kind of courage to recognize that the decisions you made repeated the patterns of finding yourself in the cycle of abuse over and over again, and an even more dazzling array of bravery to cut those chains and recognize that you had to free yourself to live the life you were destined for.

Breaking generational cycles and battling the inequities in unjust, broken systems? #overachiever. As we begin to reflect on our lives and let the light shine in the crevices of our experiences, it can be a humbling, terrifying and courageous task. Doing so can allow us to look at the parts that are beautiful but need to be cleared of the debris. Diving deeper can illuminate the parts that need healing, repair, and fixing.

For me, the hardest part was looking at the broken pieces of my childhood and the injustice in our educational systems towards minority children while taking an honest assessment of the damage and false beliefs I entered adulthood with. It was also learning how to give myself grace. Granting myself forgiveness and grace was by far the hardest lesson to learn. When I realized that I had allowed abusive cycles to repeat in my life it hurt like hell. Forgiving myself for not advocating for what I needed when I had the opportunity to but didn't have the resources or support structures was some of the hardest lessons to learn.

And that is the crux of this book. Ignorance isn't an excuse any longer. Like the saying goes, "When you know better, you *do* better." We don't just need to do better; we *must* do better. We need to do better for our students, our schools, and our communities.

We need to learn to look at our own issues, the baggage we bring to the table, unpack it, and learn how to appropriately name the pieces that impact our present. We need to continue to have the hard conversations about racism in our schools, about corruption and abuse of power within school systems, and about the invisible children who are abused and neglected behind closed, unaccountable doors.

When the final chapter of a read-aloud would end and our beloved characters were parting ways, my Sparkling Scholars always realized the striking power of taking the lessons we learned, the revelations that were illumined, and using the motivating power of love to drive us forward. While we shared in the tender pangs of having to say goodbye to the characters that felt like friends, we realized that it would do the book or author no justice if we didn't take what we learned and use it to make the world a better place, better at least than how we found it. We realized that with every reading of the words, "the end," even as tears may have streaked down our faces or we rejoiced in seeing a book come to a just conclusion, that "the end" was truly just the beginning. The real work began in our hearts as we sought to take what we learned and be agents of change, bringing hope to a world that so desperately needs it.

ACKNOWLEDGEMENTS

This book would not be possible without standing on the shoulders of my amazing tribe that have loved me and taught me all that I know about life, g(race), and education.

To my precious boys who lived part of this story with me. Thank you for the privilege of being your mom. You have shown me what it means to love, and to fight for what is worth fighting for. Thank you for being uniquely you and teaching me the lessons I needed to know to be the best mom and teacher I could be. I love you.

To my grandparents who loved me, raised me, and gave me a beautiful childhood: thank you. Thank you for showing me the beauty of unconditional love and acceptance, thank you for everything you gave me. Your imprint and impact on my life made me who I am today.

To Julie, the sister I prayed for and always wanted, thank you. Thank you for walking through this story with me, every step of the way. Thank you for encouraging me to keep on writing when I felt like the passion for this project had died. Thank you for your artistic spirit, your quirkiness, and your passion for creating. Your dedication to reminding us both to be unswerving in our dedication to emotional health, and your passion for Black Lives Matter. Thank you. I'll love you forever.

To my cheerleader, Katherine Black. Your enthusiasm and joy for this project has been contagious. Knowing you were cheering me on, kept me motivated when my writing waned, and I needed encouragement to keep going.

To my fellow teachers and colleagues throughout the years, I acknowledge you. You have collectively shared, taught, laughed with, and cried with me throughout the years. You have shown me what it means to collaborate, to love children and families who were hard to love at times. You have shared the best practices, theorists, and your candy stash with me. Your passion for your craft has inspired me and impacted my own craft. I am who I am today because of your mentorship, your desire to make our schools a better place, and your unswerving dedication to your students. Thank you isn't enough.

To my mentors, families, students, and fellow survivors helping me to understand the complexities of racism and systemic injustice, thank you for your vulnerability. Thank you for sharing your experiences and for answering my questions. Thank you for challenging me and allowing me the honor to hear your stories. Thank you for being the teachers I needed and for your patience as I learned and continue to learn. Thank you for showing me how to be a survivor and for your lessons in resilience. I would not be where I am today without all of you.

Made in the USA
Monee, IL
08 July 2022

99304351R10146